# Disrupting Temp Labor

# Disrupting Temp Labor

## A SMARTER WAY TO MANAGE VARIABLE WORKFORCES

**Paul Baker**

ISBN-13: 9781086008845

Typeset by Amnet Systems.

# Table of Contents

# Forward

n 1995 I had the privilege to serve with a number of exceptional leaders in the transformation of a twin Nuclear Power Station in Virginia. The results of our 18 month effort were nothing short of amazing, yet accomplishments are fleeting. In spite of the bureaucracy and tedium of the nuclear industry, I learned a great deal about the principles how a team of peers with different authorities and responsibilities can achieve greatness through aligned incentives, servant leadership and process discipline.

Inevitably, our accomplishments led to our downfall, most if not all members we promoted and reassigned to build and lead new teams solving new problems. Alas, our new culture faded away faster than it was born. To build and maintain a culture both good and bad requires work. This work is distributed over a long time, it is a campaign not a project. It does not require perfection; it requires humility, persistence, experimentation, trust, fairness and most of all learning.

Over the course of the next 10 years my professional career took me to various corners of the globe, different industries and through operations and executive positions in an effort to recreate my profound experience of 1995. To my chagrin, a culture of greatness cannot be bought, it is grown.

In early 2006, all the planets aligned and the opportunity presented itself to form a company centered on my three principles of teamwork (1) aligned incentives, (2) servant leadership and (3) process discipline.

This book is how we apply our principles to a market segment served by Productiv Inc. Principles born out of necessity in the Nuclear Power Industry and thriving in the Packaging and Fulfillment Industry.

Rich Boehling
CEO and Founder of Productiv, Inc

# Acknowledgements

n 2016, my business partners, Brendon McGann and Doug Legan, and I set out to build a better entry level and variable labor program for manufacturing companies. After our own experiences in manufacturing and the military, we spent a year interviewing Ops and HR leaders, at Plants and at HQs, to understand their biggest pain points, and all the tactics they were trying to overcome the typical challenges with managing a large, entry level and in some cases highly seasonal workforce.

One of those interviews turned into an important introduction for us. A former colleague and friend of mine, Rick Fulton, introduced us to Rich Boehling and Louis Sabetti, founders of Productiv, Inc, who in their words 'set out with the same goal in 2006'. Back then, they were looking to reverse the commoditization of the entry level workforce. In the subsequent 14 years, along with their senior leaders who we've been privileged to team up with, Marius Ailenei, Alan McNamara, Larry Yarborough, Chris Bullock, Jason Rowley, Alvina Gonzalez, Rodrigo Hammett, Willi Estrella, Zach Gladbach, Chris Lee, Val Tunnell, Ian Tunnell, Tice Schenkel, Elsie Rodezno, Laurie Marker, Susan Dennis, Virginia Belcher and Lisa Manning, they developed and codified *The Productiv Way* of signature lean processes. These are described in Part 2 of this book along with DIY strategies for interested readers.

Since 2016, we have teamed up to scale this approach throughout the manufacturing and distribution industries in order to turn waste into productivity for capacity constrained clients. If you're in this camp, we hope you find this book useful and will reach out to share your story and compare notes.

Thank you to Lisa Manning who provided the project management to get this book to the finish line, to Patrick Boardman for his help with layout and design including the cover and to Jessica Churchill, Churchill Creative, for the white board graphics throughout the book. Finally to Cory Bray for laying out the process for me to get this book off the ground.

# INTRODUCTION

# Let's do a 3x on Human Productivity

## A Mindset Shift From Reducing Labor Cost to Increasing Throughput

In the 1990s, 2000s and 2010s, technology in manufacturing has been about how to cut labor costs. Everything from replacing humans with machines to replacing full time employees with temps was implemented. In the 2020s and beyond, we have an opportunity to change the story to be about how technology is driving output and enabling creativity. This change of perspective in our expectation is of usage of technology is going to come down to whether or not humans and robots can operate together in a collaborative environment or not.

And this isn't about whether Robots and Humans can get along in the HR sense of the word. This is about whether ROI's are higher for purchasing collaborative robots or replacement robots. In that equation, there are a few variables that we can plot with certainty. On the robots side - they will become cheaper and their performance will improve. On the human side - we will become more expensive. The only variable that we aren't sure what will happen to is whether or not human performance will improve, stagnant or decline. So our goal is to drive human performance up and in doing so, make the case for collaborative robots over replacement robots. Robotics has the opportunity to become a great employment generator.

## Turning Waste Into Productivity

The good news is that whether you believe that or not, there is no downside to increasing productivity today. This book is about how to increase productivity in order to bring the cost of man down. Whether you are pro or anti-robot, we all will benefit from turning waste into productivity. In the this book, we will show ways to double, triple and in some cases 10x human productivity without robotics. So whether we stand a chance against the robots or not, we will at least make it an epic fight.

Corporate HQ around the world are in a constant evaluation of how quickly the ROI payback can be of purchasing machines to replace employees. As soon as the cost of a machine equals that of an employee, the machine will likely win. So the cost of robots is going down and with minimum wage hikes and the skills gap in the manufacturing workforce, the cost of man is going up.

So if we hope to avoid a mass dislocation in the manufacturing workforce, or at least push it off into the future as far as possible, then we must bring the cost of man down. If wages are going up - then our only option is to increase productivity which we have lagged at doing in our current business cycle as Productivity has lagged beyond prior periods.

As Aragon in <u>Lord of the Rings </u>says "*A day may come when the courage of men fails, when we forsake our friends and break all bonds of fellowship. But it is not this day. An hour of wolves and shattered shields when the age of Men comes crashing down! But it is not this day! This day we fight!*" So yes, the day will come when robots replace most or even all of our workers. But it is not this day!

# Part 1

## We Broke the Labor Model

# CHAPTER 1

# How Did I End Up Managing a Plant Full of Temps?

## Overheard at your company:

*The General Manager:* "We have to order 30 temps just to get 15 to show up"

*Dept. Manager:* "Our temps typically only last 2 or 3 days before quitting"

*Supervisor:* "The new temp never returned from lunch"

*Purchasing:* "Corporate approved adding a 4th staffing agency."

## Sound Familiar?

Do any of these situations sound familiar to you?

- You and your leadership team have reduced the requirements for new hires down to "we just want someone who is dependable, will show up every day and isn't lazy"
- You have contracts with two or more staffing agencies and still have trouble getting people
- You no longer have trainees on each piece of equipment ready to take the place of a retiring operator and worry a little more each year the problem is getting worse

If so, then you may also have made a similar transition that many companies made coming out of the Great Recession away from hiring employees and instead using temporary labor to keep labor expense to a minimum.

## How We Got Here

Corporate HQ was preaching the need to match revenues and expenses and there-fore GMs at plants had to move to a temp labor staffing model in order to flex with production on a weekly, or even daily, basis. And as they matched daily revenue and costs, it was having the unintended consequence of driving up the long term costs in a complete shift of altering the cost profile of the plant as the lower productivity of temp labor extended change-overs and run lengths and created bottlenecks in finish-ing of which the impacts reverberated throughout the production cycle. Temp labor becomes a crutch and once in place, it becomes very difficult to go back to hiring full time employees at the entry level.

When referring to 'bringing in temps' I am excluding 'temp to perm jobs.' Many companies successfully use temp programs to 'test drive' new employees for 90 days and then promote to full time. What I am referring to are the usage of large amounts of temporary labor for both one-time projects and ongoing unskilled work that is characterized by seasonality, demand surges, manual labor and uncertain customer order patterns. The types of temp jobs where there is no full time job at the end of the road.

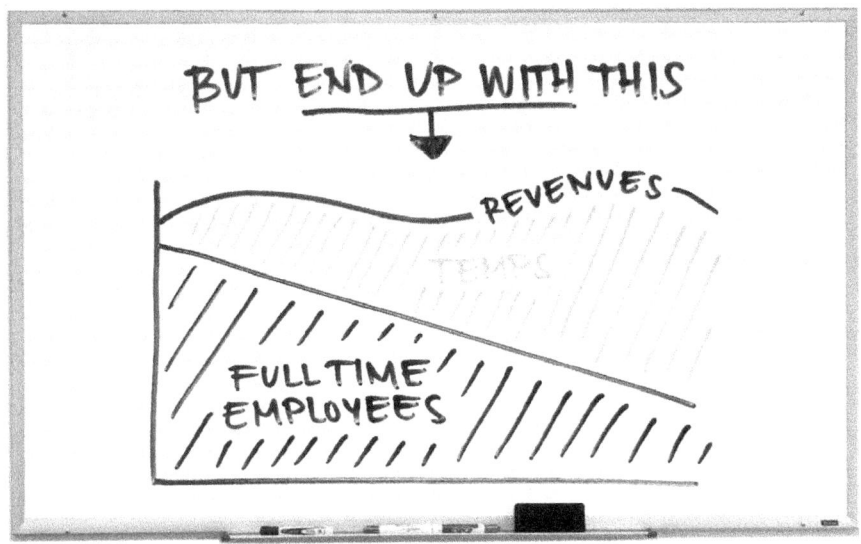

## Staffing Agencies and Misaligned Incentives Can Perpetuate The Broken System

There are 20,000 staffing companies in the US that operate 39,000 offices in the US alone, and the staffing industry doubled from $81 billion in sales in 2009 to $161 billion in 2017.

The model of using temporary employees is increasing while within this growing market is a decline in employer-employee loyalty going in both directions. Companies don't commit to temps and temps don't commit to companies. It's a broken system where the most vulnerable members of our workforce, temps without experience, enter into a workplace where there is no training, no valued work, no upward mobility and in many cases, no one takes the time to learn their name.

Remember your first day of work, and how nervous you might have been, imagine going through that experience monthly at the entry level. And while some staffing agencies do a great job servicing clients and developing employees, the norm is a commoditization of our entry level workforce doing a disservice to all involved.

The staffing agency temp model charges a fixed mark-up on top of the hourly wage of the placed temp. This model is a misalignment of incentives between the staffing agency, client and employee as shown through common scenarios in this table:

| SCENARIO | CLIENT IMPACT | STAFFING AGENCY IMPACT |
|---|---|---|
| **Not Enough Temps Show Up** | • Production throughput declines<br>• Work schedule shifts | No impact |
| **Temps moving at slow pace** | • Labor costs rise<br>• Production throughput declines | No impact |
| **Temp Quits After 5 Days** | • Operators get frustrated<br>• Retraining new person begins | Send in next Temp |
| And where misalignment is the most severe: | | |
| *More Temps Needed* | *Labor expenses rises* | *Revenue and Profits rise* |

At the end of the day, a staffing agency increases their revenue and their profit by placing more temporary workers with their clients. This unfortunately is misaligned with clients who are trying to reduce their labor costs by using less input per unit of output. And caught in the middle is the temporary employee who is looking for a full time job where they can build skills that are valued in the labor market.

## No Good Options

Even with robotics and automation, Operations Managers are still going to have a need for manual labor. Traditional options are to hire full-time employees (FTEs) or to use temps - both of which come with pros and cons. And sure, some of the cons could be due to economic factors such as the unemployment rate, but for the company doing it right -- the Employer of Choice in an area -- finding good people is seldom a challenge. In this book we will talk about ways to get there.

## Empathy for Temps:
## Would you Take this Job?

**Wanted: Packers**

**Job: Temporary**

- Compensation: At or near minimum wage
- 40 hours per week not guaranteed
- Won't be called in if there is no work but must be willing to show up every day just in case there is
- Job responsibilities will include anything that the full time employees do not want to do
- Onboarding program will consist of showing you where the bathroom and break rooms are
- Won't bother to learn your name
- No training program for future advancement
- Will be work directly with an annoyed operator who no longer will take an interest in you since the last 3 people quit after he/she spent a week training them on the process

Oh, and:

- Must demonstrate pride for the company, can't make quality mistakes and must show strong work ethic

## Summary

- Manufacturers must be able to match revenue and labor costs in order to stay profitable and competitive
- Manufacturers have relied on staffing agencies providing low skilled temporary labor to do this
- The costs of using temporary labor can far exceed the hourly wage charged by staffing agencies
- Staffing agencies are incentivized to place as many people and work as many hours as possible whereas manufacturing companies are trying to use as few people as possible
- There is a better way for manufacturing companies to match their revenue and labor cost

## Take Away Tool: Temp Turnover Rate Calculator

Most of us can calculate our turnover rate for FTEs. And depending on the economy, it typically ranges from 5% - 15%.

For a plant with 100 employees, we usually have 5 - 15 employees leave voluntarily and be replaced each year. While this is an important metric as replacing key employees can be both expensive and difficult, have you ever thought about calculating your Temp Turnover Rate? Sometimes we don't think of this as important as our employee turnover.

And while typically temps are doing jobs that are easier to replace, and have a shorter learning curve, our TTR might surprise you as it may be even more disruptive to your operation than you'd expect.

| TEMP TURNOVER RATE (TTR) CALCULATOR | |
|---|---|
| Average # of Temp Positions in Plant (X) | 30 positions |
| # of Temps That Worked in Plant past 12 months (Y) | 280 |
| Temp Turnover Rate (TTR) | = X / Y * 100 = Temp Turnover Rate % |

Yes, if you just did this exercise now, you may realize that your TTR might be over 500% and even over 1,000%. And yes, that rate might be 100x your full time turnover rate. Can you imagine if that were your full time turnover rate? Let me help you. For those same 30 positions, using your full time turnover rate of 10%, you would have had 3 people leave and be replaced. Compare that to the 280 in our example. That is 93x worse. We've become so accustomed to the broken labor model that we operate our sites and entrust our customer's products to a major part of our workforce that has a 1,000% turnover rate.

Our full turnover calculator can be found at **http://www.uptimeworkforce. com/?project=turnover-rate-calculator** which includes breakdowns by shift, skill and tenure.

# CHAPTER 2

# The Huge Hidden Costs of Temp Labor

## Overheard at your company:

**Procurement**: *"Good news, we were able to get the staffing company mark-up down to 28% by giving them a national deal at that rate."*

## Stop Looking at the Mark-Up

You get what you pay for is a very appropriate saying when it comes to entry level workforce. Most procurement departments measure success based on lowering the staffing agency mark-up. Enabled by a shared belief in operations that staffing is a commodity, margins are being pushed so thin that staffing agencies themselves have difficulty devoting resources to an account that has thin margins.

## The Total Cost of Using Temps

While the savings from having fewer employees is easy to quantify, the costs of replacing employees with temps that can be ordered daily from a staffing agency are much higher than most expect or plan. The cost of bringing in temps extends beyond the hourly rate charged by the staffing agency. That is just the tip of the iceberg. But we look at that rate because it's easy to identify and typically the rate that finance matches to the budget when doing budget variances. Though the full hit to Net Income should include the following:

1. **Direct Dollar Costs** – Financial
   a. Excess overtime
   b. Additional rework
   c. Lower productivity
2. **Indirect Costs** – Culture
   a. High turnover
   b. Upset operators having to train and retrain
   c. Low work ethic
   d. Not developing a bench of skilled operators
3. **Indirect Costs** - Management time
   a. Badging
   b. Scheduling
   c. Discipline
   d. Time card approvals

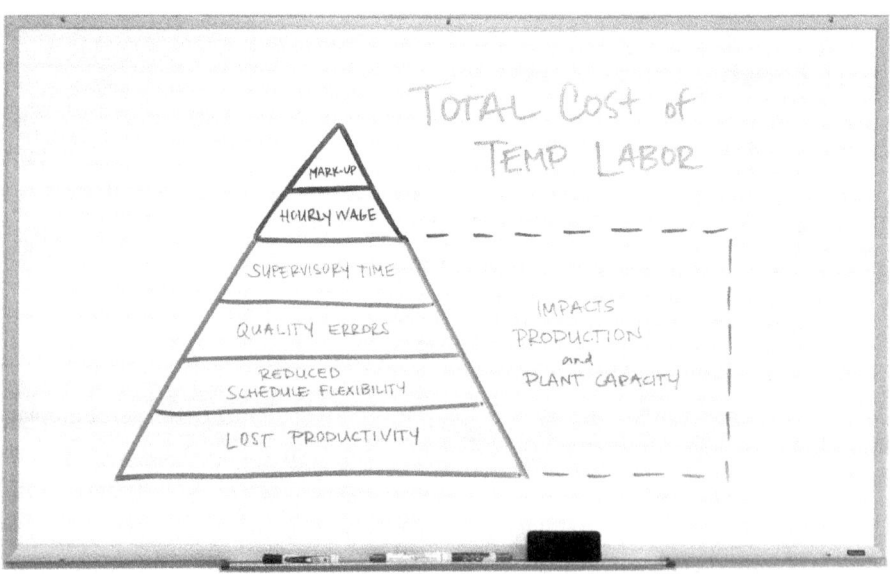

## What Wage are you Really Paying?

Looking beyond the mark-up is an important part of looking at our labor costs. While mark-ups typically range from 30 - 50% on top of the hourly wage, we are missing 50% of the cost of temp labor.

In this tool below, we look at the cost of the Productivity Gap between highly productive "good" crews, planned crews and less productive "weak" crews.

| | | Good Crew | Planned | Weak Crew |
|---|---|---|---|---|
| **Job Size** | *total units* | 50,000 | 50,000 | 50,000 |
| **Run Speed** | *units/min* | 20.0 | 16.0 | 12.0 |
| **# People on Line** | *# of packers* | 12 | 13 | 15 |
| **Burdened Labor Cost** | *$/hour* | $15.00 | $15.00 | $15.00 |
| **Downtime** | *percentage* | 2% | 5% | 10% |
| **Days to Run Job** | *# of days* | 5.2 | 6.5 | 8.7 |
| **Manhours to Run Job** | *# of hours* | 510 | 711 | 1,146 |
| **Cost to Run Job** | *total $* | **$7,650** | **$10,664** | **$17,188** |
| **Cost Per Unit** | *jobs/year* | $0.15 | $0.21 | $0.34 |
| **Implied Wage Rate** | *$/hour* | $15.00 | $20.91 | $24.18 |

*We have benefits deriving from the Good Crew and additional costs and issues from the Weak Crew. A lot comes down to - what are the costs of taking 8.7 days to complete a job that was planned at 6.5 days and that a Good Crew can run in 5.2 days? Below are some key differences between good and weak crews.*

| | GOOD CREW | WEAK CREW |
|---|---|---|
| **Freight** | Can optimize freight with additional 1.3 days to ship | Will it need to go expedited in order to meet customer delivery time? |
| **Overtime** | Not needed - finished early; may reduce OT on other jobs in freed up time | Will you need OT to cover the additional 2.2 days needed for the job to ship? |
| **Scheduling** | Picked up 1.3 days in the production schedule that can be used to get ahead on other jobs | Behind 2.2 days will likely need to shuffle |
| **Indirect Labor** | Free up time for material handling and supervision | Additional time needed for material handling and supervisor |

| | GOOD CREW | WEAK CREW |
|---|---|---|
| HR | Recruit fewer people | Need to recruit more people with more turnover |
| Rework | Minimal with good crews will catch rework likely in line or at QC | On average will have more and more likely it will be caught at shipping, at customer or in the field |
| Customer Impact | Will receive on-time or early. Can adjust to last minute changes if needed | May receive late with loss of flexibility to accommodate any supply chain changes |

## Where the Hidden Costs of Temp Labor Are On a Typical Day

When we pay our staffing agency for labor instead of output, we have to pay wasted time throughout the day.

- Lost 15 mins at Shift Start because we requested 30 temps but only 25 showed up. Reshuffle schedule.
- Tomorrow we'll request 35 to compensate....but we could potentially overpay for five.
- Lose 15 minutes to re-setup the job that didn't finish yesterday
- Lose 60 minutes training the new team members who will start today, but who might quit before the end of the week
- Lose 15% of production for the new team members to learn the job they were just taught
- Lose 25% of production due to work ethic

**Keep in mind**: These aren't individual 15 and 60 minute losses. They are multiplied across the entire job team, and dependent teams.

## Doing The Math: Hidden Costs in Action

Remember, the learning curve is at least 1 week of doing the job, so the value of a temp on day 6 is a 3x multiple of a day 1 temp. With the typical temp turnover ratio that can be 500% - 1,000%, many times we don't get through week 1 and so our temp labor force never gets up the learning curve to performing at the levels that meet our standards. Think about how effective you were on your first 3 days of a job versus how you perform now.

## Summary

- Temp labor, and all unengaged employees, can have a much larger financial impact on your plant than merely their wages
- Costs from temp labor show up as direct financial costs but also indirect financial costs as their impact can ripple through the plant
- In addition to reducing productivity and therefore negatively impacting the financials, poorly run temp labor programs can also have detrimental cultural effects

# CHAPTER 3

# Improving and Innovating on this Model

### Overheard at your company:

*Operators: "I trained the last two temps and they lasted a week. I'm not going to go through the hassle of training the new guy as he'll be gone in two days anyways"*

### Sound Familiar Again?

The operators stopped training the temps because they turned over too fast. And now even when we get a good new helper, no one bothers to learn their name, onboard them or train them. This commoditization of our entry level workforce has repercussions well beyond the entry level and unskilled positions. Many companies use temp-to-perm programs to identify full time personnel, and while some do a great job of identifying and cultivating talent, others sit back and wait for some to 'rise to the top'. The issue with the latter approach is that companies are overlooking and losing access to many great employees by merely looking for diamonds in the rough.

### How To Do It

Whatever solution we choose—employees, building a part-time Flex labor force, staying with temps, or outsourcing to a group like Productiv—the ultimate goal is the same: increase productivity while reducing cost of our manual labor workforce.

The next section will discuss definitions of Lean, Servant Leadership and Gainshare. Many of these terms have become overused and mean different things to different people and therefore we'll define each to set the foundation for the remaining chapters.

## "Commoditization of our entry level workforce has repercussions well beyond the entry level and unskilled positions."

## Lean

When referring to Lean in this book, we are describing the continuous improvement mindset that aims to reduce or eliminate waste in all areas of the production environment. The idea of waste in lean goes beyond physical waste and deals with the 7 types of waste as outlined in the Toyota Production System published for the first time in 1992.

The steps we discuss could all be considered 'Lean' as our ultimate goal is to increase throughput while reducing the cost and time to achieve it.

## Servant Leadership

Servant Leadership is a management philosophy focused on removing obstacles for our employees. Unlike a hierarchical leadership philosophy where the focus is on how can the workforce serve upper management - in Servant Leadership, the focus is on how can management serve the workforce.

We believe the workforce is who makes the money in a business on a day to day basis. They are the ones that run the equipment, liaise with customers and work as a team to accomplish tasks. Therefore, our job as servant leaders is to remove all of the obstacles they face in accomplishing this mission

## Gainshare

Gainshare is the program in which additional corporate profit is achieved due to additional performance from the workforce and is paid out. As opposed to Profit Sharing, where the total profit is split amongst all who participate in achieving it, the Gainshare pool is based on over-performance. Typically the gainshare component is a higher percentage of a smaller pool. It is set up this way so that the workforce wage achieves the expected profit and the gainshare component benefits both the shareholders and the workforce.

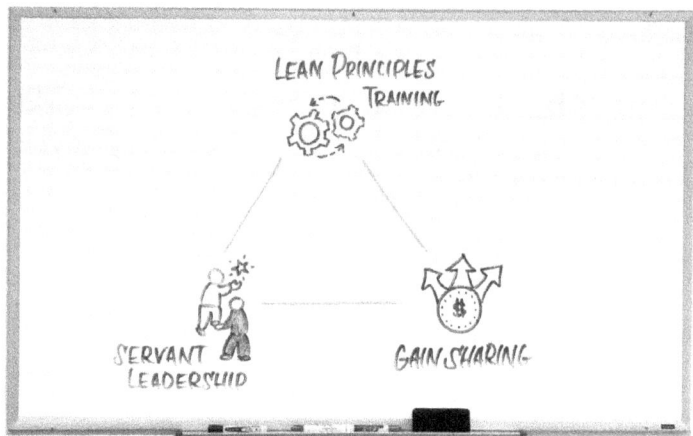

## This Book – Parts 2 And 3

This book introduces one way to achieve these goals using a combination of Lean Principles and Servant Leadership while wrapping a gainsharing program around it to tie to financial performance. Part 2 will dive into the components that make up this methodology and Part 3 will provide a guide on how to find an outsource partner if you decide that DIY isn't at the top of your priority list but still want to make massive improvements in this area.

## Summary

- There are multiple options to innovate and improve in the traditional temp labor arena
- The one we will discuss in the following chapters was developed over time and through much trial and error by Productiv and combines lean, servant leadership and gainsharing

# Part 2

## DIY – How to Set Up An Efficient Hand Packaging and Kitting Operation

# CHAPTER 4

# Baselining Your Cost Per Unit Metric

## A quote to keep in mind:
*"You can't improve what you can't measure"*

## Why Cost Per Unit

Cost Per Unit (CPU) is to manual labor production such as kitting and assembly what OEE (Overall Equipment Efficiency) is to equipment based production. When comparing CPU to OEE, the main difference is that in CPU we are targeting a cost baseline while in OEE we are targeting an efficiency baseline.

CPU is valuable for these reasons:

1. It lets us know real time profitability of a job
2. It gives us our baseline cost for considering alternatives such as automation or outsourcing
3. The metric adjusts immediately which gives us the ability to get instant feedback on line adjustments, mistakes and improvements

While we will use CPU as our main metric, it is complemented by safety and on-time delivery. For this book, we will focus on CPU and how to use it to increase throughput while reducing cost.

## Calculating the Formula

CPU is an easy metric to get on the production floor. The formula for cost per unit is:

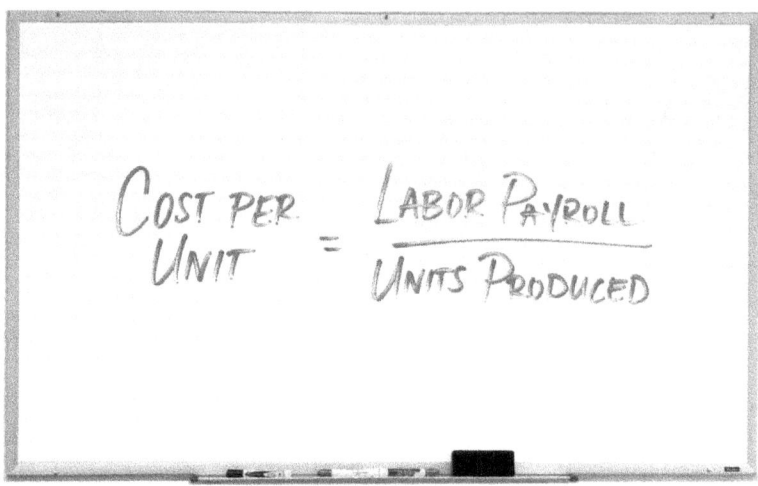

*Labor Payroll*

To calculate labor payroll, we are looking for the burdened cost of an hour of work. The burdened cost of labor being the actual cost including the hourly wage, benefits and taxes.

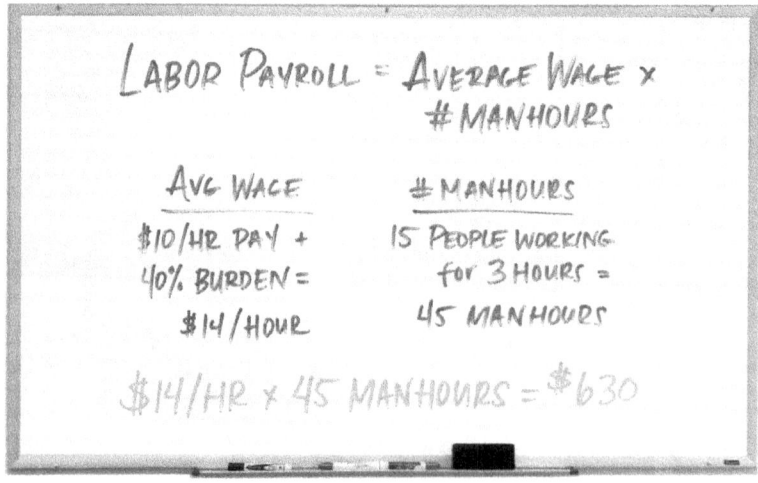

To calculate average wage, a good rule of thumb is to increase the hourly wage by 40% to cover taxes and benefits. For instance, if we have 15 people people working on a job who make on average $10/hour, let's use $14/hour as the average wage.

To calculate # of manhours - we count the number of production workers involved in the project. If we have 15 people working on a job for 3 hours, # of manhours = 45 (15 people x 3 hours = 45 manhours). What is important here is that we need to calculate the 3 hours as total hours as opposed to merely working hours. In other words, manhours must include downtime if the line stops for any reason during production.

So 15 people working an 8 hour shift at $14/hour would make Total Payroll 15 x 8 x $14 = $1,680.

### Units Produced

Calculate # of Units Produced on a 'per SKU' basis and only count 'good units' that meet quality specifications.

So if during the 8 hour shift above, those 15 people produced 5,000 good units of SKU 1001, then our CPU would equal ($1,680 / 5,000 units) or $0.34 CPU.

## The Value of Knowing Your Cpu

Now that we know the CPU is $0.34 for SKU 1001, we can use that as our standard performance measurement. Perhaps we want to measure CPU for SKU 1001 across different shifts, or different teams. Perhaps we want to set a goal for our teams to get to $0.29. They can go about doing this by either (1) increasing throughput per shift (units produced) or (2) reducing the number of people on the line (labor payroll). We'll talk more about these two ways to achieve lower CPU in subsequent chapters.

## Cpu and the Shift to Output

When you know your CPU, you can shift focus away from hourly wages and staffing markups to OUTPUT. What good is bringing in temps at a lower wage than full time employees if you have to use 50% more people, or take twice as long, to get the same amount of work done? Our data finds that unskilled workers can have a productivity variance of 300%! We'll discuss why this variance exists in a later chapter.

Here are two ways to illustrate this point using the following example whereby our client wants us to produce 5,000 units. We have three different crews of 10 people at our $14/hour average wage who will run this job, a Strong Crew, Fair Crew and Weak Crew.

This example illustrates how variable manual labor work results can be and therefore why this is worthwhile to focus on to drive meaningful savings.

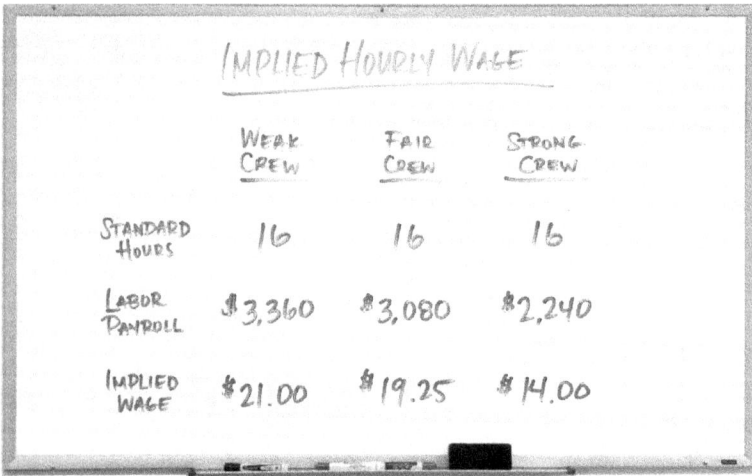

Look at the chart above and see how a Strong Crew can generate 33% savings producing 5,000 units. In the second chart, we see calculations for an implied wage. While we were focused on bringing temps in at \$10/hour and getting the markup on our staffing agency as low as possible, we are actually paying \$21.00/hour for that team.

> "We should be focused not just on hourly wages and staffing mark-ups, we should be primarily focused on OUTPUT."

## The Full Picture: Indirect Costs, Materials and Downtime

In addition to the production CPU, we also have a number of indirect costs that we won't consider as part of CPU but need to take into consideration when we look at our total costs. These include:

1. Supervision and Quality
   a. The supervisor's time in managing the work
2. Material handling, Shipping, Receiving
   a. Fork truck driver's time to pick and stage orders
   b. Cost of the fork trucks and/or pallet jackets
   c. Material handler time to restock the line with components
   d. Material handler time to remove dunnage
   e. Cost of packaging waste - corrugated/plastic (offset by any recycling revenue)
3. Quality & Rework
   a. Rework rate on this SKU
4. Human Resources
   a. Recruiting, hiring, badging for security
   b. Onboarding and training
   c. Turnover
5. Learning Curve
   a. a. Productiv's data show that there is a 300% difference in productivity between new employees and those who are up the Learning Curve
6. Downtime
   a. Changeovers
   b. Non-production minutes

In the next section, we will discuss how to lower our CPU. We have many levers to pull and we will categorize them into two main buckets:

1.  Increase # of good units per hour
2.  Reduce manhours in:
    a.  Production
    b.  Make-readies
    c.  Downtime

## Take Away Tool: Cpu Worksheet
**A Typical Day and the CPU Metric:**
We have 12 people working today. We pay our staffing agency $14/hour. The shift is 7:00am - 4:00pm with one hour of unpaid breaks, hence eight hours of potential productivity.

Here is our daily production schedule for the day.

| SKU | # OF UNITS DUE | # OF UNITS COMPLETE | TIME PRODUCED | # OF PEOPLE | MAN-HOURS | CPU |
|---|---|---|---|---|---|---|
| SKU A | 1,000 | - | - | - | - | - |
| SKU B | 3,000 | - | - | - | - | - |
| SKU C | 5,000 | - | - | - | - | - |
| Here are our results for the day | | | | | | |
| SKU A | 1,000 | 1,000 | 7:00 - 9:00a | 12 | 24 | $0.34 |
| SKU B | 3,000 | 3,000 | 9:00a - 12:00p | 12 | 36 | $0.17 |
| SKU C | 5,000 | 5,000 | 1:00 - 4:00p | 12 | 36 | $0.10 |

## Every Minute Counts
You'll notice in the above that the Time Produced accounts for every minute of the shift. This is important if we are to capture our Total Labor costs. We can't just start the first time produced once the line starts.

For instance, one area where many companies see leakage is start times. If the shift starts at 7:00am but the line doesn't start until 7:10am, we need to account for those 10 minutes somewhere in our CPU metric. For a plant with 100 people at

$14/hour working 24/5, the annual cost of those 10 minutes is $175,000. So we can pick up $175,000 of cash and profit just by having our teams start on time.

There are many places where we see "Minute Leakage" throughout the day. We'll identify these and provide solutions in subsequent chapters.

## Summary

- The first step in implementing any continuous improvement program is to baseline our current metrics.
- For hand packaging and kitting, Cost Per Unit (CPU) is an easy, real time figure that we can use to measure performance.
- When we look at CPU, we must include not only our production time, which can be expressed as CPU for each SKU, but also downtime and make-readies.
- In addition to our workforce manhours, there are also numerous indirect costs that should be taken into consideration such as supervision, material handling, human resources and the learning curve.

# CHAPTER 5

# Getting to a State of Flow - JIT, SPF & Conveyors

## A quote to keep in mind:
*"I wish we didn't have to run a 2nd shift but we can't get all the work out during 1st shift"*

## In The Zone

It goes by many names in different arenas of human performance. In sports we say that a player is "in the zone." In manufacturing, we say we get our teams into a state of Flow. Flow is that state when production starts on the dot at 7:00 am because everyone showed up and was at their station at 6:59 am with all the materials pre-staged from the night before. People work at a pace that isn't fast nor slow but rather smooth. The tasks have been made simple enough so that the day flies by. Those times when even a General Manager can take some time to go out and grab lunch. You know those days. They usually happen only once in awhile. But there is a set process to follow to make them happen every day. The way we do this is by implementing a simple Just in Time strategy for 'what' and 'when' to produce and then a Single Piece Flow process on a Conveyor for 'how' to produce it.

## Just in Time Vs Just in Case

Typically Just in Time (JIT) is the goal we strive for when discussing how to lower our inventory as much as possible. The aim being to reduce costly 'safety stock' storage and only hold materials needed for immediately upcoming production -- you know, to free up working capital. And while this is definitely important, remember that JIT goes far beyond inventory and is in fact a supply chain and manufacturing strategy. For example, when we apply JIT thinking to Finished Goods, it is about only producing the goods for which we have customer orders and delivery dates. As tempting as it is to convert raw materials into finished goods so we can 'be ready' for orders, this temptation represents the opposite of JIT. Therefore, in our scheduling process, choosing what and when to produce is just as important as deciding how to produce.

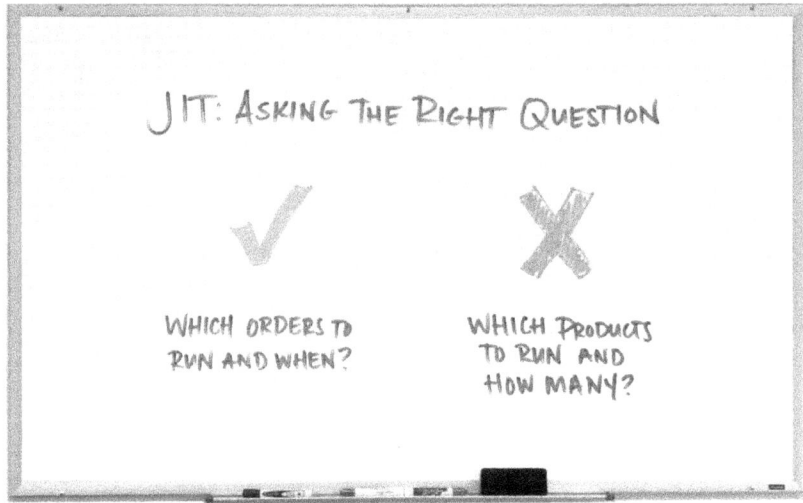

Contrast JIT with what we call 'Just in Case.' Just in Case is about producing items that might be purchased in the future but where no customer orders currently exist. On first look, this seems to make some sense -- if we have capacity, why not go ahead and build and store for the future, right?. You know -- increase our 'utilization' and our 'efficiencies'. The reason we want to avoid Just in Case is that it is solving the wrong problem.

Our problem isn't what to do with extra capacity, our problem is why do we have so much extra capacity? Our job as managers of production isn't to find things for our workforce and equipment to do each day. Our job is to receive, produce and ship customer orders while using the least amount of cash and operating expense to do so. If you want an in-depth and humorous look at optimizing capacity, check out Eli Goldratt's, *The Goal*.

## Is JIT Against Human Nature?

Productiv founder Rich Boehling had an interesting insight regarding inventory storage and human nature. After reading the book *Sapiens* by Yuval Noah Harari, Rich hypothesized a connection between our desire to store large amounts of inventory with the evolutionary human instinct to store food to guard against future scarcity.

If this connection exists, then in order to move to JIT we have to develop a sound process *AND* we have to overcome some of our basic instincts to 'plan for a rainy day.' One way to make the shift to JIT is to have a disaster recovery plan whereby we test supply disruptions to our JIT system and iterate through solutions such as having multiple vendors, or qualifying multiple vendor locations that produce the needed products.

## Single Piece Flow

Once we schedule our production based on the customer orders and delivery dates we have in house (instead of scheduling based on capacity), the next step is to produce those orders by processing and building one unit at a time. This is called Single Piece Flow (SPF). SPF has a positive impact on both throughput and quality. To see this in a simple demonstration in action, take a look at this **video** from the Gemba academy and see how doing single piece flow reduces envelope stuffing time by 21% from 3:44 mins to 2:56 mins. No increase in cost or effort but a 21% labor savings. Why? Because there is no inventory waste and no motion waste from building piles. Instead of completing each step of the envelope stuffing process (fold insert, place insert in envelope, lick and stamp envelope), the builder does one envelope from start to finish before moving on.

To see another example of how SPF increases throughput, view this **video** from TheLeanWorkshop.

The opposite of Single Piece Flow is batch production. Batch production is where we start and finish each step of the production process for the entire batch before going on to the next step for the entire batch. As you may have seen in the 2nd video mentioned above, one issue with batch production is that it creates downtime for the other steps in the process.

## Moving to Conveyors -- Throughput Benefits

When looking at JIT and SPF in a hand work environment such as kitting, assembly or gang run pick pack, we use conveyor belts to enable SPF. Typically we are moving away from batch production which is done on tables and known as "Table Builds."

*Pictured: Conveyor Belt Set Up (Left) vs. Table Build (Right)*

## Moving To Conveyors *(Continued)*

Using conveyor belts improves productivity and quality by enabling single piece flow. Here's how:

- Speed of production is set by the Line Lead as opposed to being set by each individual. Think of the line lead as the coxswain in rowing. One person sets the pace for the entire boat as opposed to letting each person decide the speed at which they want to row.
- Conveyor belts prevent WIP build-up during the assembly process.
- Each station is dependent on the prior station. Therefore, there is a quality check at each station prior to job execution.

## Quality Benefits

There are multiple quality benefits of using single piece flow as well, and specifically conveyors versus table builds. We look at a real-world example at the end of this chapter to explain the quality benefits of conveyors such as:

- Reduced error rate
- Reduced time doing quality control
- Reduced re-work

Each of these benefits leads to additional throughput because workers spend less time doing QC and re-work and more time producing output.

Let's compare SPF on conveyors to batch production using table builds:

| CONTINUOUS SPF - CONVEYORS | STATIONARY BATCHES - TABLES |
|---|---|
| Each step in the process is done in line and only occurs after the preceding step is completed | Each step in the process is done independent of the other steps |
| If there is an error - all production stops | If there is an error - have to go back and determine which boxes were affected |
| Multiple redundancies to catch a missed or repeated step | Single point of failure to miss or repeat a step |
| All team members contribute to each finished good | Team members only see their specific task |

## Why Quality Improves When Using Conveyors Versus Tables

One of the most prevalent quality issues with handwork is missing components. In the below example, we look at handwork quality which typically means does the finished good have:

- Right quantity
- Right components
- Right place
- Right amount of time

Imagine you are in charge of assembling a kit with 8 components in it. You have two ways to accomplish this: using a conveyor belt or using a table.

> "The less time we spend doing QC and re-work, the more time we have for production."

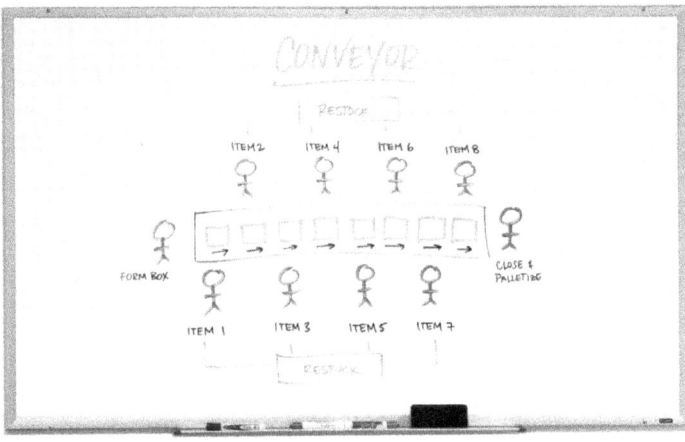

## Using a Conveyor Belt:

In this scenario, you create eight component stations and each station is in charge of putting one item or component in the box. The first person in line makes a box and places it on the conveyor and then each person inputs their component into the box. The person putting in component #2 doesn't take that action until they see component #1 in the box. The person putting in component #3 doesn't take that action until they see component #2 in the box and so on. At the end of the line, one person checks to make sure all items are in the box and then closes, tapes and palletizes it. Boxes are started and finished one at a time without stopping at any point in the process. This is Single Piece Flow.

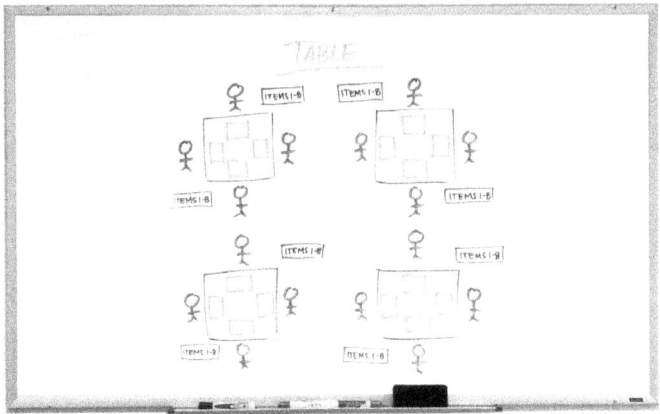

*Using a Table:*
In this scenario, you prebuild all of your boxes and line them up next to the table in a giant stack of boxes. And then you have all of your components on the table. Each person stands at the table, grabs a box and starts putting in all eight components themselves. That person then closes and tapes the box and puts it on the pallet. A QC person then picks out boxes throughout the process, opens them up and checks them to make sure all the components are inside.

*Comparing:*
The conveyor method is doing quality 'in-line' because it is done while the boxes are being assembled and not offline, or off the assembly process, which costs more money, takes more resources -- labor and floorspace. By the time the box makes it to the end of the conveyor belt, all eight people only acted when the preceding person acted and the person closing and taping the box took a final look. And what is great is that when items are put in the same location, it becomes a visual indicator for all eight people on the assembly line of what the box should look like and where the pieces fit. Everyone becomes a quality inspector.

Compare this to the Table Build where only one set of eyes was on each box and if someone happened to stop paying attention when they ran out of a component and started making boxes with only their seven remaining components, then the short will never be found unless QC randomly picks the shorted boxes. Your client will likely get boxes with missing or duplicate components and the only way to rework the job will be to take them all back and visually inspect each one. Humans aren't perfect. We get tired and can zone out. Therefore we must create processes that take this quality risk *off the table*.

Further, when we look at the restock and material handling process, the conveyor method allows restock from both sides whereas the table method requires multiple drop offs which weakens the process by:

1. Increasing labor
    a. Each of the 8 stations needs all raw materials so we have to sort before restocking
    b. Have to manage 8 individual drop offs instead of just 2 stations

2. Increases quality errors
   a. a. Instead of replacing 1 SKU with 1 SKU, allows for mixing of components
   b. b. Reduces ability to do line clearance during changeovers

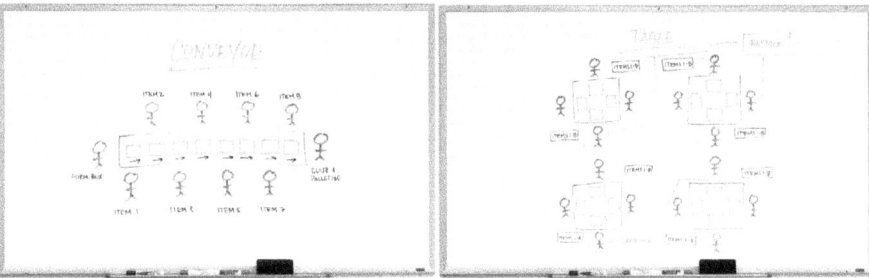

*A side-by-side look at the Conveyor Set Up vs. Table Build models*

## Summary

- To get to a Flow state of production, we first must move from Just in Case to Just in Time. We need only to produce the items for which we have received customer orders.
- Once we have our schedule set, our production method should be Single Piece Flow, i.e. start to finish on one item before starting the next item. We don't stop our work in process. Items must be completed if they are started.
- The best way to enable SPF in hand packaging is to use conveyor belts.
- In addition to improving throughput, using conveyor belts and SPF also improves our quality by preventing errors and reducing rework (if there are errors) by easily identifying the impacted products.

# CHAPTER 6

# Staffing the Right Number of People

## A quote to keep in mind:
*"We have to request 30 people to make sure we get 20 because if we don't have all 20 we have to shut the line down for the day. It kills our on-time delivery and slows down production."*

## Benefits of Smarter Staffing

Traditionally, we decide our staffing levels on the number of manhours needed to complete a job. This manhour figure is likely accepted as tribal knowledge after years of doing certain jobs, or it's a conservative estimate for new jobs. We use this approach, and then one of two things happens:

1.  Our estimate has a ton of fluff in it since the staffing for handwork is unreliable. In this case we will beat our estimates, but will likely lose the work on cost.
2.  Our numbers are too aggressive and we will win the work, but lose money on it. Fortunately, there is a smarter way.

We can staff our lines based on the number of operations and the speed of the conveyors. When we do this properly, we can sharpen our pricing to win new work, and we'll know we can optimize the line for profitability.

## How to Set the Right Staffing Level

So how do we determine the number of operations? Go ahead and build the product yourself, and count the number of operations.

> "When we do this properly, we can sharpen our pricing to win new work"

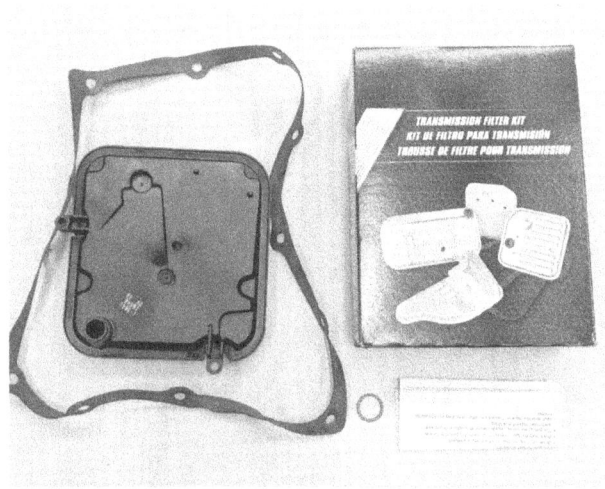

| OPERATION | # |
|---|---|
| Build the box | 1 |
| Place the print insert into box | 1 |
| Insert the filter into box | 1 |
| Insert the O-ring into box | 1 |
| Fold the gasket | 1 |
| Insert folded gasket into box | 1 |
| Close the box and tape it shut | 1 |
| Place box in master carton | 1 |
| Palletize master carton | 1 |
| Total Operations: | 9 |

So now that we know the number of operations, we can easily figure out the right staffing level as we aim to set an equal level of effort for all operators.

# 1 Person 1 Job

If you've ever watched a machine perform a task, it is done one operation at a time. As a component flows through the machine, each station performs one task. For instance on a cartoning machine, one set of arms pushes the flaps in, a second set folds the top, a third applies glue, a fourth tucks in the top and a fifth pushes out the carton to make room for the next.

We can follow this model using people, the world's most dextrous and flexible machine. '1 person 1 job' is a good rule of thumb to staff a line and it has two main benefits:

- Increase in line speed
- Improved product quality

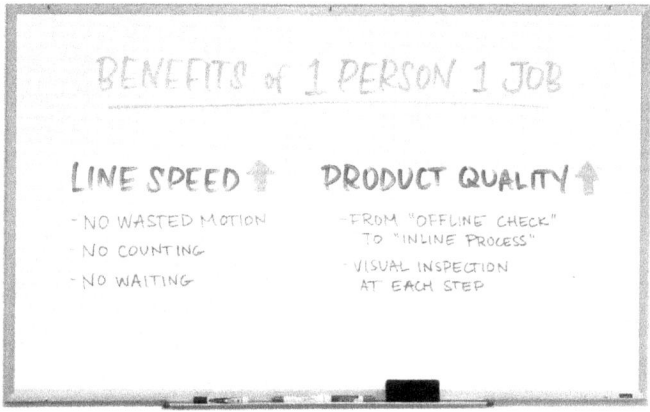

Here's how it works to reap the benefits:

1. Each person focuses on one item without needing to wait, count or make decisions during each operation (imagine counting to 3, eight thousand times in one day)
2. Turns quality control from an 'off-line check' to an 'in-line process' and provides a visual, independent check on each job

That's it. Yes, this is possibly the easiest concept in this book you can use to increase productivity. Match 1 person with 1 operation. Combining what we've learned so far, we will have a 9-person team working on our conveyor belt.

Before you think I'm crazy for having 9 people work on a small job, I'd like to convince you why 1 person 1 job is less expensive than having multiple people do it. And, if I can't persuade you here, I encourage you to try it on your own shop floor.

Imagine your job is to package 4 components into the retail carton mentioned above. If you use 4 people to do this work (instead of 9) the set-up will look something like this:

| HYPOTHETICAL 4 PERSON LINE SET UP | |
|---|---|
| Build the box | 1 |
| Place the print insert, filter and O-ring into box | 1 |
| Fold and insert the gasket into box | 1 |
| Close the box and tape it shut, place in master carton and palletize | 1 |
| Total:    4 People Doing 9 Operations | |
| | (Mismatch) |

What's wrong with this example? A few things:

1.  It is much faster to build a box than it is to put in 3 components. So the person putting in the print insert, filters and o-rings will have a large pile of boxes waiting for components. The box maker will have to take frequent breaks to wait for space to put new boxes.
2.  Grabbing 3 items and putting them in a box is going to have a lot of motion for the packer and likely is going to get pretty tiring by the second half of an 8-hour shift.
3.  The second person (folding and inserting the gasket) can't easily peek into the box and identify that it has an insert, filter and o-ring already, and therefore we are losing a valuable quality check.

So how could we improve on this 4-person set-up? We can produce this finished good for a lower unit price and with better quality by using 9 people to package the goods where each person is in charge of 1 operation. The benefits of this are:

1.  Increased line speeds in a balanced manner:
    a.  No wasted motion
    b.  No counting before acting
    c.  No waiting on previous actions

2. Quality improves
   a. Visual inspection of 1 component from preceding station
   b. Consistent placement zone

# What to Do With Too Many or Too Few People

So what do you do if you don't have the right number of people? Here are a few ideas:

## Too Many People

This is a potentially large problem since we are adding substantial cost to our daily operation.

1. Additional Packer: Are any operations more difficult than others? Are there areas where 2 people could do one operation? For instance if folding the gaskets takes a long time, consider having 2 people fold gaskets and increase the line speed
2. Material handling: Is material handling and dunnage a major factor for these jobs? Could an extra material handler reduce downtimes as a result of stock-outs for the station?
3. Set-up: Can an extra person do make-readies and line clearance, thus mini-mizing change over time and freeing up time for the Leads?

We also need to avoid setting a staffing level that results in having to send people home – and avoid sending leads home at all costs. It is tough enough to find great people and when we have them, the cost of paying them for a day is much cheaper than the cost of replacing them. Of course, if you haven't scheduled properly, then you may not be able to afford to keep extra people onsite. Fix this issue upstream as quickly as possible as it is much easier to add flexibility into the schedule than it is to find a great team member.

## Too Few People

Having too few people is much more stressful than having too many people because it can start to impact on time delivery, production capacity and supervisor time since they will spend more of it fighting fires.

1. Slow down the production lines. To maximize throughput, don't try to run the same jobs at the same speeds with fewer people. You will risk quality errors and tire out your teams. The best way to salvage throughput is to slow down lines and keep it smooth.
2. Leads and supervisors need to get on the line.
3. Do the short-run jobs. This may seem counterintuitive, but change-overs are less expensive when you are short people. So knock out your short run jobs if you can on the days you are short staffed.

## Doing the Math: More People Can = More Profit

WAIT! It is cheaper to use 9 people for a job that we were doing with 4 people?

YES! It's all about FLOW and here is the math to prove it:

Let's use our previous example where we are hand assembling 5 components into a finished box, putting that box in a master carton and then palletizing it for shipment. We have 20,000 units to complete. The table at the top of the next page compares the job staffed with 9 people versus the job staffed with 4 people.

|                      | STAFFED WITH 9 PEOPLE | STAFFED WITH 4 PEOPLE |
|----------------------|-----------------------|-----------------------|
| # of people          | Staffed with 9        | Staffed with 4        |
| Unit Speed           | 25 units per minute   | 6 units per minute    |
| Units per hour       | 1,500                 | 360                   |
| Total hours needed   | 13.3 hours            | 55.6 hours            |
| Burdened Payroll     | $126/hour (9 x $14)   | $56/hour (4 x $14)    |
| Total Cost           | $1,680.00             | $3,111.11             |
| Cost per unit        | $0.084                | $0.155                |

Increasing from 4 people to 9 people will increase production by 316%. In our tests, we had throughput go from 6 units per minute to 25 units per minute. A 316% increase. If you had to do 20,000 units, then the smooth line would do this work in 13.3 hours while the 4 person line would do it in 55.6 hours. This 76% decrease in time to completion will greatly help our scheduling department while the 46% decrease in cost will greatly help our finance department!

Why does this happen? Because there is no waste and no stress. We replace the wastes of motion with productivity. 9 people without any unnecessary motion or setting items down can move more than 4x faster than half as many people doing multiple things, and with better quality.

## Summary

- The standard method for determining staffing levels is to look at manhours required for a job. This method may work for some projects but it is not optimal for hand assembly work.
- Instead, we should set our staffing needs by looking at the number of operations needed to complete a job.
- We should set our staffing need by this rule of thumb: 1 person 1 operation.
- Once we know the number of operations for each of our finished good SKUs, we can start designing our staffing plans at least 1 day in advance based on tomorrow's schedule.

# CHAPTER 7

# Setting the Right Speed for Maximum Throughput

**Overheard at your company:**

*GM:* "Why does the line keep stopping?"

*Lead:* "We weren't going to hit our production targets today so the supervisors increased our line speeds."

In an effort to increase throughput, our instincts tell us to increase line speeds. This is ironic because we know that setting a machine to run too fast will result in bad quality. For some reason, however, we think humans just need to put in more effort to go beyond their max speed.

So when using a conveyor belt to set the work speed for our teams, we think: faster belt = more units per minute, and more units per minute = greater throughput. Unfortunately this common practice couldn't be more wrong since increasing run speeds often has the opposite effect. High speed can wear people out while creating stress in the system. The result is more line stoppages and more rework.

Let's discuss why faster does not equal more throughput, and then we'll look at how to set the right speed to maximize throughput while maintaining quality.

## The Treadmill Thought Experiment

A quick thought experiment based on running on the treadmill at the gym: You head to the gym to run 5 miles. You get on the treadmill and once you hit Quick Start, the belt slowing starts to move at a barely noticeable 1.0 MPH.

At this rate, you will neither get your work out nor be home in time for dinner. A speed of 1.0 MPH would take 5 hours to run 5 miles. So naturally you start to increase the speed to something comfortable, say 5.0 MPH. At this pace, a 5 mile run will take 1 hour and you'll go home with a nice post-workout feeling. So let's agree that increasing the speed from 1.0 MPH to 5.0 MPH does in fact reduce the amount of time to complete your workout.

What if we increase the speed from 5.0 MPH to 10.0 MPH? Now we only have to work out for 30 minutes to run 5 miles. So we start running and after 5 minutes we are out of breath and now we have to slow the belt down to 4.0 MPH for a few minutes to catch our breath. Then we try again and we only make it at 10.0 MPH for 2 minutes this time. So we slow down the belt to 4.0 MPH to catch our breath again. We do this on and off a few times until we are exhausted and decide to just finish our run at 4.0 MPH. After 45 minutes, we are exhausted and get off the treadmill at about 3.5 miles.

So it's easily illustrated how going faster does not mean finishing faster. Take this thought experiment a step further and imagine you now do this same exercise 5 days per week, Mon-Fri all year long. What is more sustainable - a nice 5.0 MPH run consistently every day or the ups and down of starting at 10.0 MPH and switching back and forth to 4.0 MPH? For most, this is not an enjoyable way to exercise.

"High speed can wear people out while creating stress in the system. The result is more line stoppages and more rework."

## Setting the Right Speed

Setting the right run speed is all about smooth Flow. As we like to say "fast is slow and smooth is fast." Finding the right conveyor speed is an iterative process. We try different speeds until we find the speed that maximizes our throughput, minimizes the workforce stress and maintains required quality levels. Here is the process to set the right run speeds:

**Step 1**: Start the conveyor belt at a slow pace in order to begin the flow of product and you'll notice a few things:

    a.    People will be standing around and waiting on the box in order to do their operation

    b.    There will be large gaps in between products

**Step 2**: Increase line speed slowly until people begin working at a normal pace and look for:

    a.    Boxes arriving at each person's station just as they finished filling the previous box

    b.    The large gaps between products will shrink

    c.    If you are going too fast, you will see:

        i. Product begins to pile up at one or more stations

        ii. People are reaching forwards and backwards to grab product

**Step 3**: Eliminate the piles by doing one of the following:

    a.    Slowing the line speed down

    b.    Add a person at the bottleneck stations

    c.    Make the job easier by changing the motion or adding a jig

**Step 4**: Iterate. Repeat steps 2 and 3 until you are in a state of Flow without piles, waiting, sweating and quality errors

## Why is Setting the Right Speed so Important

Setting the right run speed is important because speed is the key leverage point for:

- Staffing with the right number of people
- Meeting customer delivery schedules
- Running the operation profitably
- Eliminating overtime
- Eliminating without quality errors
- Reducing workforce turnover

There are few red flags to look out for that signal we may have the speed set too slow or too fast:

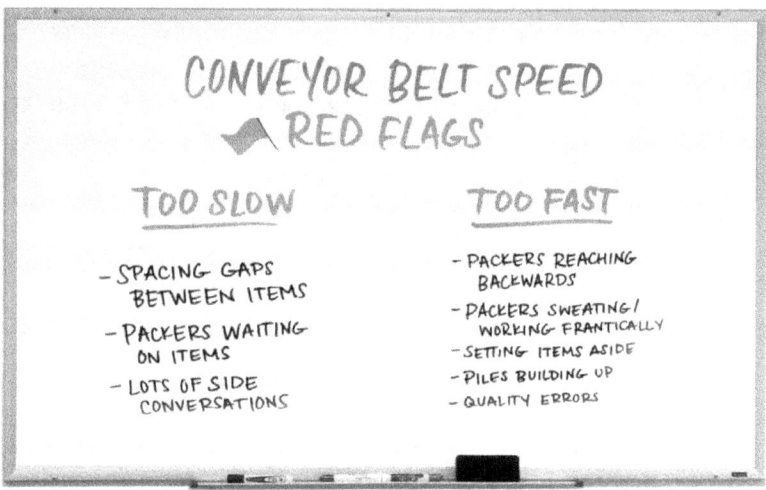

While setting the right speed and Flow is just one step in running lean, it is the step that has the highest leverage to the outputs we are trying to achieve.

## Doing the Math: Slow Down for More Throughput

Imagine we have a 100,000 piece job that had been taking us 8 hours to do but we are getting pressure from our general manager to reduce labor expense, so we have to go faster.

Therefore, instead of running at our typical 12,500 pieces per hour to hit our target, we turn our speed up in order to be able to do 15,000 pieces per hour.

Read on to the next page to see what happens:

- At 15,000 pieces per hour, each person has to work 20% harder to do the same job that we set to the optimal standard already
- People immediately start to fall behind, and every 4th item gets pulled from the line and returned to start because the speed is too fast for the team to keep up

- If the goal is 100,000 items, then we'll have 25,000 items that will get pulled from the line and will have to go through at least a portion of the process twice

At 12,500 pieces per hours conveyor speed we did the job in 8 hours. At 15,000 pieces per hour conveyor speed we did the same job in 8.3 hours with these negative consequences:

- We had to add a person to the line in order to take the sidelined products back to the start of the line
- We had 0.3 hours of overtime because the job had to get out
- Everyone left exhausted and disappointed from an extremely stressful day at work

So if you set the speeds right the first time, the only way to get more production is to change the process or add more people, the former always being preferred to the latter. We'll discuss some ideas on how to change the process for more production in later chapters.

## Summary
- Setting the conveyor speed is the key factor in meeting customer delivery schedules, running the operation profitably, eliminating overtime, staffing with the right number of people, executing without quality errors and reducing turnover.
- Setting the conveyor speed to an optimal level is an iterative process that requires watching for visual cues.
- When the conveyor speed is optimized, no one will be waiting for the next item (too slow) and no one will be frantically trying to keep up with the pace (too fast).
- Faster speed does not mean more throughput. Smooth FLOW is the key to more throughput.

# Take Away Tool: The Lean Red Flag Watch (RFW)

**The Lean Red Flag Watch (RFW)** uses trial and error get to the point of maximum productivity, highest quality and easiest work for your teams.

Conveyor Speed Calibration (CSC)

| RED FLAG | TOO FAST | TOO SLOW | FIX |
|---|---|---|---|
| **Piles building up at each station** | X | | Break down the role at that station or add a 2nd person to do the work |
| **Packers reaching** | X | X | Increase speed or decrease spacing among packers |
| **Setting items to the side to catch up on later** | X | | Slow down the line! |
| **Quality errors** | X | | Slow down the line and ensure 1 person 1 task |
| **Packers sweating** | X | | Slow down the line or else team will get burned out before the shift is over |
| **Packers talking to each other** | | X | Speed up the line |

# CHAPTER 8

# Ergotivity

**A quote to aspire to:**

> *"Wow. I've never seen a team work like this before."*

To increase throughput, we've discussed the importance of '1 person, 1 job," and setting the right line speed. To sustain optimal throughput, we're introducing the concept of "ergo-tivity" in this chapter.

Ergotivity is a phrase coined by one of our leaders, Lisa Manning, to mean supercharging productivity while making the work ergonomically easy. We fine tune each position and process to reduce wasted motion, increase throughput and reduce packer fatigue.

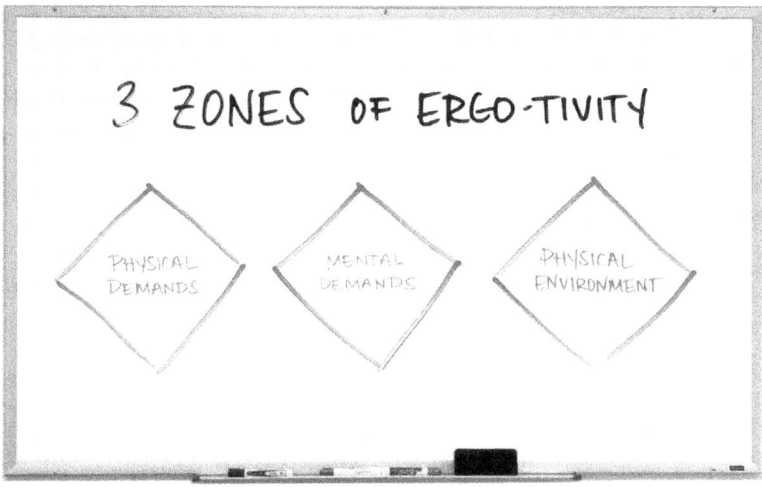

*There are three focus zones of ergotivity: Physical demands, mental demands and the physical environment or facility. Let's take a look at each zone and the opportunity to improve ergotivity and hence throughput in each.*

## Making the Work Easy: Physical Demands

Have you ever stood on an assembly line for 8 hours and packed boxes? It is incredibly difficult work. It is tiring, tedious and stressful on our muscles and joints. Some jobs are more tedious than stressful (inserting components into a box in the middle of the line). And some jobs are more stressful than tedious (taping and palletizing boxes at the end of the line).

It's the leaders job to make the work as easy as possible for each team member through ergonomic design and creating a comfortable environment. The good news is that not only is this the right thing to do, it also prevents injuries, promotes a safe workplace and drives profitability.

When looking at the ergonomics of packing jobs, we want to begin by targeting and eliminating the following wastes of excess motion:

- Reaching (as discussed with run speeds)
- Turning (having components staged behind you on the line)
- Walking (refilling components)
- Lifting (using tools)
- Bending (component table too low)
- Twisting (switch body position)

While creating good ergonomics on a packing line seems obvious, I rarely witness it in practice. However, ergotivity done well has massive benefits. The ROI on moving staged components closer to someone in order to prevent reaching is probably the best investment you can make in a plant.

Nowhere else can 30 seconds of manual labor return thousands of dollars of productivity, yet 90% of managers who walk past poorly staged components or an ergonomically disadvantaged line don't make a change.

Ergotivity Checklist

| MOVEMENT | FIX |
|---|---|
| **Packers reaching side to side** | Increase speed or decrease spacing among packers |
| **Packers reaching up or down** | Conveyor at wrong height. Adjust speed or provide step with safety markings to shorter team members |
| **Turning** | Stage components on tables next to or above for picking items |
| **Walking** | Move carts and components closer to where they need to be |
| **Lifting** | Arrange tables to reduce lifting distance |
| **Bending Over** | Put a cart in place |
| **Standing on concrete** | Anti-fatigue mats |

## "Moving staged components closer to someone... is probably the best investment you can make in a plant."

Optimal line speed also contributes to reducing physical demands. As discussed earlier in this chapter, line speed should be set so that no one is stressing, reaching, turning or making any unnatural movements.

The speed of the line is the ultimate lever on ergotivity and the easier we make the work on our workforce, the faster the line can go without sacrificing quality.

## Making the Work Easy: Mental Demands

In addition to the physical demands, we also want to simplify mental demands such as excess counting or mental math. Asking someone to count out 10 components before inserting them seems very easy to a manager when drawing up a quote. I challenge you to try counting to 10, 5,000 times in one day looking at the same objects.

Anything that requires calculations, counting or visually searching needs to be re-engineered. For instance, instead of one person counting to 10, can we use a weight scale? Or could we create an offline station that pre-packages components into bundles of 10? Instead of visually searching for components at our station, can an upstream worker place the components in the same location each time?

# JIGS

In order to reduce both excess physical and mental strain while maintaining quality, we can create jigs. A jig is like a template or device that holds a piece of work and guides the tools operating on it. It's purpose is to create repeatable accuracy. We should always be asking "how can we create jigs to reduce the number of operations or calculations to make it easier for our teams?"

You may already have a dozen jigs located all around your plant. They are those small tools your inventor maintenance guy builds to solve equipment problems. I am suggesting that you can apply that same ingenuity to your assembly line.

## Making the Work Easy: Physical Environment

A comfortable work environment matters for two main reasons: (1) We don't want people to be uncomfortable while working (too cold, too hot, too dark, lights in eyes) and (2) unlike the physical and mental demands of an assembly line, the environment typically impacts ALL workers, even the big boss. So, we want to ensure a clean, comfortable and safe environment to increase everyone's productivity.

Sometimes we don't have full control over the work environment.

For most of you reading this book, your teams will be working in a manufacturing plant or warehouse environment. Within that environment, we can't always control every environmental factor, but there are many ways we can improve the environment like temperature, air quality, lighting and scheduling. A comfortable environment includes:

- **Proper temperature**
  a. If your facility is too hot, consider:
     i. Warehouse standing fans
     ii. Overhead fans
     iii. Opening doors in facility to facility air flow
     iv. Cold water and Gatorade®
     v. Extra breaks
     vi. Relaxed dress code
  b. If your facility is too cold, consider:
     i. Keeping doors closed
     ii. Closing dock doors when not in use
     iii. Revisting the dress code

- **Floors**: Consider putting in anti-fatigue mats if you have concrete floors. Make sure no equipment is leaking any fluids such as oil that can create slipping hazards, and keep floors clean of debris such as shrink wrap or broken pallet pieces.
- **Air quality**: some processes like working with certain raw materials or having baling equipment onsite can create massive amounts of dust. Therefore, dust collection systems or enclosing certain areas with their own room and air quality systems will not only improve the air quality for breathing, but also keep customer products clean.
- **Building quality**: things like leaking roofs and peeling paint create a depressing atmosphere and contribute to apathy. Do whatever is possible to fix roof leaks, and consider a new coat of paint if needed.
- **Lighting**: maximize natural lighting by keeping windows clean and shades open. Replace broken or burnt out light bulbs.
- **5S**: organization of the workforce

## Summary

- Ergotivity is about reducing physical and mental demands, and improving the environment in which we work.
- We can reduce physical demands by arranging our workspace to limit unnecessary motion and staging the components to be packed so that workers are not reaching, bending, lifting or turning.
- We can re-engineer processes that create mental demands to sustain line speed without quality risks.
- Improving the working environment through facility upgrades or additions like fans and anti-fatigue mats can increase ergotivity, and outcomes in general.
- We can also simplify the work by using jigs and small tools to make operations easier.

# CHAPTER 9

# Designing the Gainsharing Plan

## Overheard at your company:
*"Unfortunately we didn't make our corporate EBITDA target and therefore our plant's gainshare won't payout this quarter."*

Is there anything worse than delivering that message above? Well, we can't always control corporate wide performance, but we can design a gainsharing program around it. Gainsharing is an incentive program whereby employees are rewarded for incremental productivity or cost saving measures. It's been my experience that gainsharing elicits either a joyous response or a contemptuous one. Nothing can damage morale more than an inconsistent gainsharing program - especially when a gainshare is used in place of giving raises.

In this chapter, we discuss one great way to give financial incentives to our workforce to reinforce the lean processes we have been putting in place.

## Why Gainshare is Vital
A gainshare program is vital because it provides the 'what's in it for me' when working with individuals and teams to increase productivity. It is a fair system to reward our workforce for the extra effort they are giving in order to achieve overperformance results.

Further, gainsharing is self-reinforcing. It prevents effort fatigue and it helps us retain our workforce. A good gainsharing program should add $0.25 to $2.00 per hour to base wages which in our world tends to be between $8.00 and $15.00 per hour depending on position and geography. If our starting wage is already market competitive, then the gainshare program should not only help us recruit the best employees, it will also reduce turnover while building our reputation as the 'choice employer' in the area.

Finally, by paying our teams for overperformance, we accelerate workers through the learning curve through engagement.

## The Gainshare Stakeholders

To have staying power, gainsharing needs to work for all the stakeholders:

| STAKEHOLDER | GAINSHARE NEED |
| --- | --- |
| Employees | Meaningful incentive compensation that is achievable and motivating |
| Management | Helps make supervision easier and leverages management time |
| Corporate and Shareholders | Must be paid out of excess profits. Can't risk paying out from existing labor expense already budgeted. |
| Clients | Can't increase the cost of service |

DESIGNING AN EFFECTIVE GAINSHARE PROGRAM

Gainsharing can make our lives easier, especially in a low unemployment world, by reducing the number of people we need to recruit, making that recruiting easier and lowering turnover. These benefits are encompassed in four main categories:

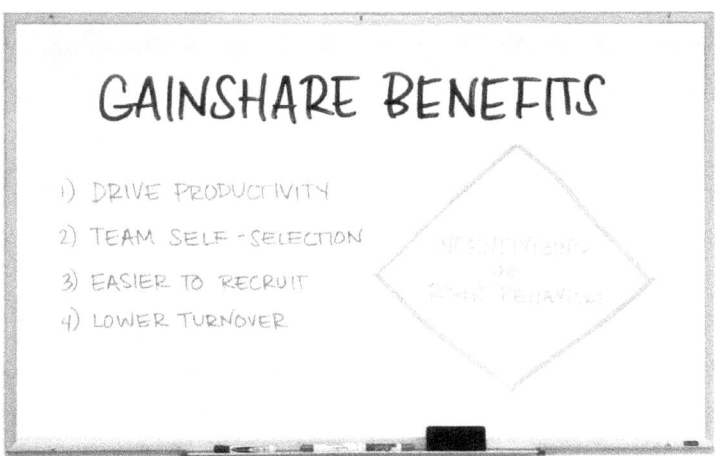

GAINSHARE BENEFITS

1) DRIVE PRODUCTIVITY
2) TEAM SELF-SELECTION
3) EASIER TO RECRUIT
4) LOWER TURNOVER

## Designing An Effective Gainshare Program *(Continued)*

When designing a gainshare program, make sure it reinforces the behaviors you want from your teams: safety, quality, productivity and throughput. Your design should take into account four main components:

1.  A set base wage plus a post-performance incentive (also called ex ante wage and ex post voucher)
    a.  Here we are trying to isolate the gainshare portion of an employee's wages to the actual 'above and beyond performance'. We should get standard performance for the hourly wage being paid plus additional productivity from the gainshare.
    b.  By isolating the gainshare portion, we are ensuring that the program is truly gainshare on the individual level. On the group level, we need to make sure the aggregate benefit of the extra production will exceed our budgeted financials and budgeted metrics.
2.  Real time feedback, a.k.a. paying a gainshare as often as 'accountingly' possible. We recommend a weekly payout.
    a.  In order for employees to tie the gainshare payment to actual work, the feedback loop needs to be as rapid as possible. Quarterly and annual gainshare programs don't have the desired impact since the payoff is too far away from the work performed. By doing a weekly payout, employees can tie exact performance to a financial outcome.

## "Gainshare helps us recruit and reduce turnover while building our reputation."

    b.  Another benefit of paying weekly is for training and engagement. For instance, when the gainshare payout is larger than expected, the supervisor can explain and reinforce causal behaviors. "Do you remember that 'jig' that Rebekah came up with that made it easier to pack the cartons? Well that saved us X man hours which went into the bonus pool." Conversely, this same coaching technique works for smaller gainshare checks. "Do you remember when we put the labels in the wrong place on the master cartons and spent 4 hours peeling and replacing them? Well we didn't get paid for that time and it came out of the bonus plan."

    c.   Finally, employees will help 'self-select' on the line. Knowing that team performance drives financial payoff, employees will encourage, or kick out, underperformers themselves.

    1.   Consistency

    a.   Use a consistent formula and metrics. And, once they are in place, don't change them! Consistency is key when designing an effective gainshare. Consistency of calculation, consistency of payout, and consistency of communication. All are necessary to build trust and credibility in the system.

    1.   Quality and safety

    a.   Finally, make sure that safety and quality are built into the gainshare program. A recordable or loss time accident should count against the bonus pool, or perhaps negate it entirely for the period. Quality should be a deduction for the actual cost of rework plus any additional costs such as additional freight to replace the product.

## Getting Corporate Approval

In order to get corporate approval, a gainshare program must be self-funding. That is, the money paid out in the program must be generated by extra effort arising from the program.

So how do we know if a program is self-funding? How do we design a program that will

1. Incent workers to increase productivity
2. Increase worker pay to be above the local market, and
3. Only be paid out of 'excess profit' generated specifically by the program?

Every corporate HQ is going to want to make sure the gainshare is truly gainshare -- that is, profit above and beyond normal production. To do this, you will need standard metrics and the budget. Only by having historical metrics can you get corporate to sign off on a gainshare. Once you have standard metrics and your budget in place, simply set your targets above the budget (and hopefully prior year) metrics and Corporate will consider that gainshare.

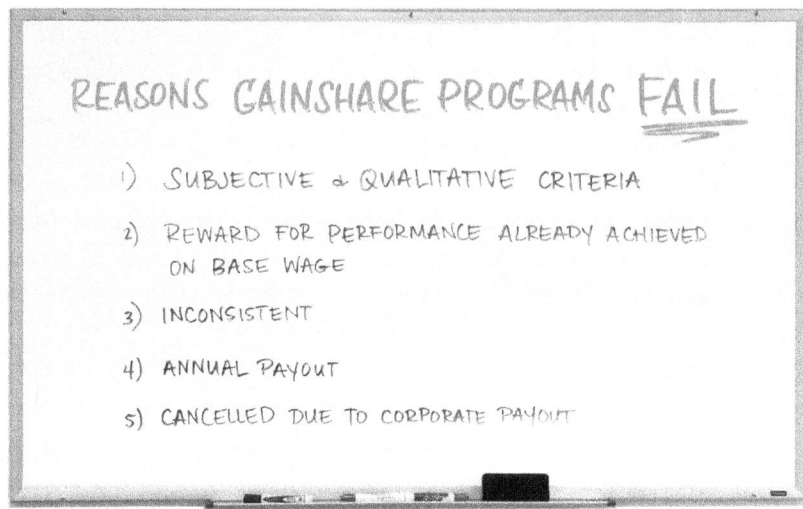

## Why Gainsharing Programs are Also Good for Your Clients

When combined with a fixed unit cost program (price per piece instead of hourly markup) clients will love gainshare programs. The client gets the benefits of:

- Increased productivity and flexibility for scheduling
- Additional capacity in finishing and packaging
- Improved quality

And they get all these benefits without additional costs. This value creation results from converting wasted time and effort into productivity and distributing the value among our workforce, our shareholders and our clients.

## Where Most Gainshare Programs Fail...Things to Avoid At All Costs

Unfortunately most gainshare programs fail to achieve the desired effect and end up in the incentive program graveyard. The reasons are varied but do come down to a few common design flaws.

## Things to Avoid At All Costs *(Continued)*

So, what do you do if your workers generated the extra push but you need that money to cover a hole somewhere else? Don't even think about it.

The damage you'll do by raiding the gainshare fund will render all of your hard work on getting to this point moot. Likely, no one will quit on you at first, but credibility and trust will be strongly eroded or lost.

## Summary

- Gainshare programs are vital to motivating and rewarding the workforce for achieving extraordinary productivity on an ongoing and consistent basis.
- A great gainshare program will have four main components:
  a. A post performance incentive
  b. Real time feedback (weekly payout)
  c. Consistency
  d. Take into account safety and quality
- Avoid the components of gainshare that typically cause failure:
  a. Programs are put in place but then cancelled due to 'corporate performance'
  b. Metrics are subjective and qualitative
  c. Rewarding performance that you'd already get as part of the base wage
  d. Programs are inconsistent
  e. Programs don't pay out frequently enough, e.g. annually
- Only put in a gainshare program if you intend to be consistent with its application and treat it like employee wages and not a discretionary fund.

# CHAPTER 10

# Building a Great Culture for Labor Stability and Consistency

## Before and After:

*Skilled Machinist:* "*I don't have time to train the temps anymore. Every time I start training one, they quit on me. After the first few, I just stopped since it's not worth it if they aren't going to be here next week.*"

■ ■ ■

*Skilled Machinist:* "*It sure is nice to be able to have John, my helper, run the machines when I go on break. Since I don't need to shut down, my production metrics are the highest they've been*"

Does the "Before" sound familiar? It's both a very reasonable and very tragic viewpoint that has become part of our everyday operation. How does a temp or new team member ever get up to speed if no one is going to take an interest in them and train them? And how can we afford to train 300 people a year if they are going to quit after 2 days?

Part of implementing the lean principles in this book is doing so with a consistent team. While the methods we've discussed in this book do shorten the time it takes someone to get up to speed and reduce the impact in skillset variability, consistency among people is still vital not only for our production metrics, but for our shop floor culture.

So how do we bring stability and consistency to our labor force? How do we reduce absenteeism and turnover while promoting good culture? In this chapter, we'll tackle 3 ways to improve the plant floor culture that go hand in hand with lean principles:

- Servant leadership
- Recognition and promoting from within
- Respect for all people

## Servant Leadership

The way we approach shop floor management is through the style of leadership known as Servant Leadership: helping those beneath you on the org chart do their jobs better. The focus is on serving down and recognizing that the production workers are the ones who make the money for the organization. To increase profits, we must remove obstacles for them to do their jobs better. The benefits for being servant leaders are numerous: lower turnover, lower absenteeism, higher productivity and a better culture.

As servant leaders, our job is to get out on the floor and make life easier for our teams. This includes:

- Giving people the right tools to do their jobs
- Simplifying the work
- Treating everyone with respect

How do we know what it takes to simplify the work? We ask and listen! Our workforce knows what they need to do a better job and it's the servant leader's job to get it for them.

## The Learning Curve - 10,000 touches

Productiv has plotted data for more than 1,000 projects to determine how long it takes for a packer to become proficient at a given task. We have determined that it takes 10,000 touches to reach 100% proficiency. No surprise, this is similar to Malcolm Gladwell's 10,000 hour rule for expertise.

So if you have temps that quit after **one or** two days, then they are only going to get to a fraction of the productivity needed to be at a maximum, and you are constantly replacing learners with learners.

Imagine an operator that is accustomed to working with the same 3 packers for over 1 year. They are proficient and productive since each has been through the learning curve. Now, imagine another operator that has 3 temp positions with high turnover. Likely, none of these temps will get through the learning curve or become proficient. So, if you hold machine OEE and operator skill constant, then you could still have a wide variance of productivity due to the tenure and proficiency of the team doing the packing.

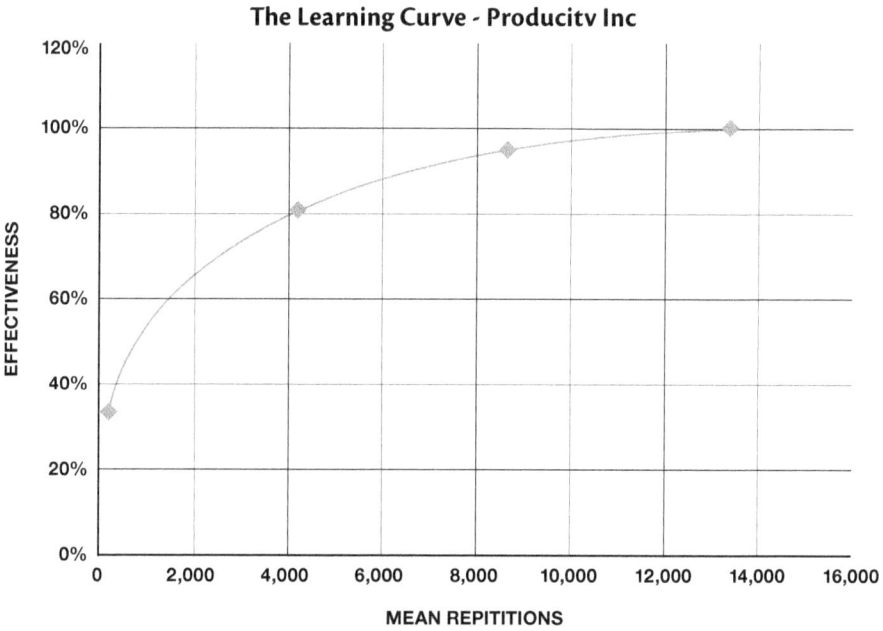

**The Learning Curve - Producity Inc**

## Recognition & Promoting From Within

There are two major question on all employees' minds:

- Am I doing a good job?
- What do I need to do to make more money?

We should have structured and 'in-line' feedback systems, recognition systems and performance management programs to answer both of these questions. While we might not be able to afford to give out a lot of raises, we do owe it to people to let them know when they are doing a good job, how to do an even better job, and what it takes to earn more money through expanded responsibility or promotion.

To build a culture of performance we must believe one thing: [almost] all workers come to work every day wanting to do a good job for us, for the company, and for the customer. If we manage teams with this belief, it is much easier to give constructive in-line feedback, to motivate performance, and to demonstrate and earn respect.

Recognizing good work is a powerful yet often underutilized motivator. Simple private or public shoutouts like thanking a team member for working on Saturday, recognizing extra effort to organize pallets, or using a pre-shift meeting to remember service anniversaries are all effective ways we can connect to people and build a great culture of respect and belonging.

Promoting from within not only rewards the person who earned the promotion, it also shows other team members that there is upward mobility. At the end of the day, having the opportunity to be recognized or advance in our careers motivates many of us. It is the cornerstone of the American Dream, and it's this motivational system that has enabled so many people to prosper in our country.

## Respect For All People

Plant floors these days are a mix of all kinds of different people. We must treat everyone with equality, dignity and respect. To be effective at building a culture of performance, we cannot tolerate racism, sexism or bigotry, and we must be unyieldingly consistent in enforcing the rules.

Our management sets this tone.

### Why we need good packers to help keep our veteran machinists happy

Skilled Operators know how fast equipment should run. And if you operate in a lean environment with production results posted, each person is going to want to be at the top of the list. So what makes an operator's job easy?

1. Properly functioning equipment
   a. Notice we didn't say 'brand new equipment' or 'top of the line equipment'. What we find is that operators just want their equipment in consistently good shape with proper maintenance and all the necessary parts.
2. Low number of changeovers
   a. a. Nothing drives an operator crazy like the scheduling department stringing a group of uncommon jobs together when some foresight could have grouped them more efficiently. Operators love to set up and just RUN.
3. A revolving door of temp labor
   a. a. Many fill lines, for example, are run by an operator and have 10 - 20 temp workers on them. These temps are doing everything from twisting on caps to hand applying labels to packaging components in cases.
   a. b. Nothing drives a machine operator crazy like having to shut down the line every 30 minutes because a temp walked off the job, someone wasn't tightening the caps properly, or a temp spilled a bottle while trying to put the cap on and now we have to clean up the line.

The Giants don't surround Eli Manning with a revolving door of offensive lineman because he'd never get into a rhythm knowing that his supporting cast keeps changing. The good news is, unlike having to pay up for offensive lineman, in a production atmosphere, we can actually save money by improving the supporting cast for our skilled operators.

## Summary

- Stability in the labor supply will increase productivity and, more important, bring calm and consistency to a plant's production.
- Servant Leadership is focused on asking 'how can I make this easier for my workforce?' through coaching and removing obstacles
- Recognition and promoting from within is critical to sending a message that good work is rewarded and that your site is worth sticking around for.
- Respect for all people is both the right thing to do and also a necessary thing to do to create a culture of performance with very diverse team members.

## Take Away Tool: Career Progression

Having a set career path with known rates of pay can help motivate all members of our workforce. Here is a diagram of what a career progression might look like that you can share with your employees.

Example Career Progression for Hand Packers

| POSITION | PAY | GAINSHARE % OF BASE | SKILLS |
|---|---|---|---|
| Packer | $10.00 - $12.00 per hour | 5% - 10% | ▪ Dependable Attendance<br>▪ Shows up on time<br>▪ Positive attitude<br>▪ Attention to detail |
| Line Lead | $12.50 - $14.00 per hour | 6% - 12% | ▪ Good reading and writing skills<br>▪ Can do basic mathematics<br>▪ Can set-up a production line<br>▪ Knows quality specifications |
| Supervisor | $14.50 - $18.00 per hour | 8% - 14% | ▪ Can balance assembly line<br>▪ Can set up a line for a new product<br>▪ Can develop line leads<br>▪ Can set up daily production to meet the job schedule<br>▪ Can maximize profitability |

| Packaging Department Manager | $18.50 - $22.00 per hour | 15%+ | <ul><li>Can manage multiple production lines</li><li>Can quote new jobs</li><li>Can work through employee issues</li><li>Coaches and mentors new leaders</li><li>Communicates with clients</li><li>Resolves workforce issues</li><li>Resolves client issues</li></ul> |
|---|---|---|---|

This chart shows the vertical progression though horizontal progression also exists to challenge operators before they are ready for a promotion. By expanding someone's job responsibilities, such as Lead 1, Lead 2, Lead 3, we can give them additional shares to raise their compensation and put them on the path towards a base wage raise when they can contribute at that level.

# CHAPTER 11

# Setting up and Maximizing the Right Metrics

## A quote to keep in mind:

*"It's great to see the P&L actually reflecting all the hard work we've been putting in."*

In Chapter 5, we baselined our cost per unit or CPU. Then we spent the latter half of this book setting up process, financial incentives and culture.

Now let's quantify the P&L benefits we should see. Once we've quantified the P&L benefits, we will discuss steps to maximize those benefits.

## The Benefits

The benefits of all our work are captured in these improving metrics on the P&L:

| P&L ACCOUNTS | METRIC | WHY |
|---|---|---|
| ■ Direct Labor Expense<br>■ Overtime Expense<br>■ Temp Labor Expense<br>■ Indirect Labor Expense | Cost per unit | ■ Using fewer manhours (FTE, OT and Temp) to produce the same output<br>■ Using fewer supervisory hours to manage fewer people |
| ■ Recruiting Expense | Turnover Rate | ■ Less turnover results in fewer recruiting ads, background checks, badging and new hire onboarding |

| P&L ACCOUNTS | METRIC | WHY |
|---|---|---|
| ▪ Revenue | Throughput | ▪ By reducing the manhours to produce the same output, we open up capacity for additional production |
| ▪ Materials | Quality Error Rate | ▪ Fewer quality errors reduces the number of manhours (FTE, temp, OT) required for rework<br>▪ Fewer quality errors reduces the number of supervisory manhours<br>▪ Less rework reduces demand on materials such as stretch wrap, shrink wrap, corrugated boxes and tape |

As Important or Even More Important - **Intangible Benefits for Leadership**

- Moving from reactive to proactive
- Less time firefighting and more time planning (Time to stop and think)
- That feeling when you come into work and the same faces are in their place, know what to do, and at 7:00 am sharp production starts.

# Cost Per Unit

In Chapter 4, we learned how to calculate CPU. And we've spent the past 6 chapters discussing ways to maximize productivity so we can minimize the CPU. Worth noting, minimizing CPU comes from reducing manhours we spend and not the market competitive hourly wage we pay our team members. In this section, we'll look at how to match up our CPU improvement with the P&L improvement.

If we have a decrease in cost per unit, then we know we've reduced our operating expenses. From the chart at the beginning of the chapter, we should see this show up in our Labor Expense categories that will all be part of Cost of Goods Sold.

| P&L ACCOUNT | IMPROVEMENT |
|---|---|
| **Direct Labor Expense**<br>• Payroll costs for the hourly workforce in production. | • Payroll costs for this segment of our employee base comes down to Hourly Wages x Hours Worked.<br>• By lowering our CPU, we reduced the number of hours worked. We should see a direct $ improvement for each unused hour this period.<br>• We need to make sure we are reducing hours worked in total (daily CPU) instead of SKU (unit) CPU since we only capture the financial benefit of fewer hours worked for the period and not just for the job. |
| **Overtime Expense**<br>• Payroll costs for the hourly workforce in production beyond 40 hours per week | • Overtime Expense follows the same rule as above for Direct Labor Expense except for two main areas:<br>1. Hours worked on a per person basis above 40 hours per week are counted<br>2. Hours are counted at 1.5x hourly wage<br>• OT Expense can be one of the highest leveraged areas of our improvement program because for every manhour we reduce using our program, we get 1.5x of financial benefit. We should aim to have $0 of OT expense. |
| **Temp Labor Expense**<br>• Staffing agency costs for providing production labor | • Temp Labor expense also follows the same rule as Direct Labor and OT Expenses. As we reduce manhours, we reduce the number of hours we have to purchase from a Staffing Agency. Like OT expense, Temp Labor Expense is also a high leverage area to target because not only do we have our workforce hourly wage, we also have to pay the staffing agency their profit. And when we use Temps for Overtime - we use an even more expensive rate as we pay 1.5x on top of the hourly wage and the staffing agency profit. |
| **Indirect Labor Expense**<br>• Payroll costs for the supervisors | • Indirect Labor Expense will work a little differently than our Direct Labor Expense as we are unlikely to want to reduce the hours of our Supervisors who typically work 40+ hours per week and are in a skilled position for us. The P&L benefit here is in reducing Supervisor Overtime. Because we can't call in another Supervisor like we can another Packer, our Supervisor core typically can have high OT as they are the only ones that can keep Production running OT and on the weekends. By reducing our manhours we are limiting the amount of OT we need from our Supervisors. |

## Turnover

Did you know your temp turnover could be 1,000% or more? It's almost as abstract a number as trying to visualize the $19 trillion US debt. So what does a high turnover rate mean? The average turnover for manufacturing plants is about 15%. So, for everyone 100 people on your staff you can expect 15 people to come and go each year. At 1,000% turnover for 100 positions, you could expect 900 people to come and go through the year. Yes, 900 people. This means that for a 5-day work week, we are hiring 17 new people each week, all year long.

While this number may seem unreasonable, it's actually not that uncommon for temp labor turnover rates to be that high. And seasonal programs can run even higher. If we use the lean and cultural concepts in this book, however, we can expect a drastic drop.

So what are the costs associated with turnover?

- **Recruiting and replacing** - Recruiting and replacing employees can typically take between 1 - 12 weeks depending on the skill level required and the local labor market conditions. For an unskilled role, we'll assume the lower end value of 1 week and $50 for recruiting and background checks.
- **Overtime** - To cover the vacant spot, other workers are typically working extra hours at overtime pay of 1.5x of wages for the 4 weeks it takes to replace the employee.
- **Learning curve** - As we saw in Chapter 10, the learning curve can mean suboptimal productivity for 1 to 3 weeks until the new employee gets up to speed.
- **Safety** - Increases in employee turnover create increases in workplace injuries. Research by the Bureau of Labor Statistics has shown increased risk of workplace injuries in the first twelve months on the job.

To summarize from previous chapters, a few ways to reduce turnover as part of our program include:

- Putting in place gainsharing programs
- Having a detailed career progression path so that team members know what to do in order to get promoted and more money
- Keeping an on-call list of pre-screened and pre-trained employees who want to work part-time
- Providing a good onboarding experience so that Day 1 for employees starts off on the right foot
- Ongoing training for people to enhance their skills

# Quality

Quality trackers look at two main sub-components: total number of errors and the total cost of those errors.

1. Our Error Rate therefore is the total number of errors divided by the measurement time period
2. Our Error Cost is the total spend of rework, freight and penalties to fix our errors

In addition to the items above we've put in place ways to improve quality such as single piece flow and in-line visual inspection. There are a few other ways to reduce quality errors:

1. Approving First Quality before starting production
2. Up-to-date work instructions
3. 20 minute quality checks done by QC or Supervisors

These three items will reduce both error rates and overall costs.

# Investing Throughput Improvements

If we improve our cost per unit, then we are using fewer manhours per unit of work. Those extra manhours go to one of two places 1) they are saved (cost savings) or 2) we've applied the hours to other areas of production. How you use the hours depends on the growth mode of your company.

| MATURE - STABLE | HIGH-GROWTH |
|---|---|
| ▪ Extra manhours are saved, results in cost savings<br>▪ Generate more cash for investment capital or new ventures to return to growth | ▪ Deploy manhours to other areas of production<br>▪ Reduce hiring burden on HR to keep up with growth<br>▪ Reduce need for working capital |

*Other Areas Where Improvements Can Add to the Bottom Line*

- **Freight Expense** - When we get behind, one lever we pull to catch up is using more costly expedited freight. By being ahead of our schedule, we can choose less expensive shipping options to get products to clients on time.
- **Repairs & Maintenance Expense** - Ever run a shrink tunnel or an ARPAC machine whose maintenance has been deferred? When we skip scheduled maintenance or defer repairs, the wasted time and materials can really add up, especially with older equipment.

## A deeper dive on throughput

We just discussed the relationship between key inputs (turnover, quality, throughput) and revenue. Let's take a deeper dive to see how being better at hand packaging can increase company revenue.

If we consider the **Theory of Constraints**, we know that bottlenecks in a plant can have an impact on the entire plant's production.

For instance, let's look at the total capacity of a printing operation by department:re, we can actually save money by improving the supporting cast for our skilled operators.

| DEPARTMENT | CAPACITY |
|---|---|
| **Order Entry** | 75 orders/day |
| **Pre-Press** | 75 orders/day |
| **Press** | 75 orders/day |
| **Hand Packaging** | 50 orders/day |
| **Total Plant Capacity** | ?? |

So how many orders per day can our plant process? The answer is 50 orders per day. We can get 75 orders through Steps 1, 2 and 3 per day but only can process 50 orders through step 4. So if 1-3 all produce at maximum capacity, then by the end of a 5-day work week, there will be 125 orders piled up at Hand Packaging that haven't been processed and shipped to customers.

So our options are:

1. Reduce capacity in Order Entry, Pre-Press and Press
2. Increase capacity in Hand Packaging
3. Outsource 25 orders per day of Hand Packaging

What happens if we can't get people into Hand Packaging from the local labor market and there are no cost effective outsource options? Then we have no choice but to reduce the orders per day going through the system by 25 in order to not end up with a mountain of WIP in front of Hand Packaging.

An imbalance in capacity or throughput is never a conscious decision we make. It's what happens after months and years of smaller compounded imbalances. Our best option is to increase productivity in Hand Packaging. By doing so, we bring our total Plant Capacity to 75 orders per day hence optimizing the capacity of our press equipment and increasing revenue.

## Summary

- What gets measured gets managed. In order to successfully implement our program we must understand where the benefits are derived and track those benefits.

- Our Program requires a lot of trial and error. Only by doing real time metric tracking can we double down on what works and move away from what doesn't.

- Our Program increases revenue while reducing our operating costs through the Direct Labor, Overtime, Temp Labor, Indirect Labor, Freight and R&M accounts on the income statement.

- By increasing capacity, we leverage not only increases in Hand Packaging but increases in capacity for the entire plant if we've removed a bottleneck.

- By improving productivity, we convert our time and energy spent firefighting into free time to use in more forward-looking and productive ways.

# CHAPTER 12

# Communicating the Results Up the Chain

## Overheard at your company:

*"Attached is the agenda for the annual budget meeting. You'll be expected to present and discuss your YTD results and next year's projections."*

A chance to present and discuss results should be an exciting time for your team. But often, it's not. Corporate always expects more than is reasonable (or possible) hence making annual budget meetings difficult to attend. But this year, you'll have some new ammunition.

If you've reaped positive results from this program, your next step will be packaging and presenting those results for senior leadership so you can parlay them into tangible benefits for you, your team and your facility. The reason you need to succeed here is because headquarters is making decisions every day about where to invest cash and where to send new work. We want to be the YES answer to all of their questions.

## Tangible Benefits To Capture

Requesting your due benefits might require Manager support -- to either grant them outright or to go to bat for them with senior leadership. In many cases, these might be things you've been asking for, but needed supporting rationale. They include:

1. Raises for the workforce
2. Bonuses for your managers
3. Promotions with raises
4. Promotions for yourself
5. Investment in new capital equipment
6. New customer work being sent to your facility

A few of these are things that corporate headquarters is always making decisions about. Those include (5) and (6), where to put new equipment and where to place new customer business.

There are always strategic items that corporate is thinking about too, like plant consolidations, closures and mergers and acquisitions. While we can't control all aspects of a multi-site or multi-division corporation, we are hugely advantaged if we are contributing great results.

## When to Communicate

While corporate beaurocracy can be out of control, and by no means are we recommending this call frequency, but if these are standing calls – go ahead and leverage the medium to appropriately communicate these results on our formal update meetings. These can include:

- Weekly operations calls
- Monthly results call
- Quarterly business reviews
- Annual budget meetings
- When the boss's boss comes to town

We should be communicating our Program process results, but should do so in the context of what the boss cares about.

"Headquarters is making decisions every day about where to invest cash and where to send new work."

## What to Communicate

We should be communicating quantitative results and then providing an explanation on how we achieved those results. For instance:

*"We improved our Gross Margin from 59% last year to 61% this year. On $2 million of sales, that improvement generated an additional $40,000 of profit during the month. We accomplished this by reducing the number of hours we used in the hand packaging department by streamlining our process which also enabled us to avoid having to work any weekend overtime as we stayed ahead of our customer's schedule."*

A good rule of thumb is to comment on the major line items of the P&L. Our boss and peers do not want to hear about how we reduced our overhead variances. People basically care about EBITDA unless your plant is one of those under-the-microscope or 'challenge' plants where folks are trying to figure out what is going wrong.

For most of what we are doing through our Program, we can use "streamlining our process" as the blanket explanation.

## Matching Our Report to Our Audience

Each of these calls has different levels of detail that our audience will care about. So we need to match our metrics and reasons to our audience.

| FORUM | BOSS CARES ABOUT | METRICS TO DISCUSS |
|---|---|---|
| **Weekly operations calls** | Customers are getting their orders on time and without overspending to produce | • Safety, On-time Delivery, Waste, Quality, and Any out of the ordinary spend items |
| **Monthly results call** | Each site is hitting their sales and profit targets and any deficient sites understand why they missed and have action plans to improve | All Major P&L line items and the variance waterfalls: • Sales, Contribution Margin, Gross Margin, EBITDA, Labor Utilization Rates, and Overhead spending |
| **Quarterly business reviews** | Each plant in the division is hitting their profit and sales targets and that any underperforming groups have action plans to make up their gaps | • Sales and EBITDA |

| FORUM | BOSS CARES ABOUT | METRICS TO DISCUSS |
|---|---|---|
| **Annual budget meetings** | The division performance and any plants that are underperforming | ▪ Divisional Sales and EBITDA |
| **When the boss's boss comes to town** | ▪ Customers are happy<br>▪ Business is growing<br>▪ Costs are going down<br>▪ General Manager is a leader who has built a strong team<br>▪ If site is performing well: details on how the GM does it<br>▪ If site is performing poorly: details on how the GM will fix it | ▪ Sales, EBITDA, and Team Leadership potential |

## How To Communicate When The Plant Is Behind Budget

It's important to remember that our boss isn't really going to care about our continuous improvement program if we are missing our sales or profit targets. When we have results that are below budget, we need to be prepared with the following information:

- P&L waterfall: a comparison of our actual results to our budget and prior year
- Explanations for all of the major variances
- Action plans for each variance
    a. What changes we will make
    b. The financial impact of those changes
    c. The timeline to achieve the changes
    d. Who is accountable for each change
- Any unknowns or additional areas that are still being investigated
    a. A timeline for answers

The amount of detail you'll be required to go into will be a good indication of how much trust and credibility you've built up. Have your plans together and be forthcoming on your fix. And most importantly, put your programs into action as fast as possible. Because by the time you understand the problem, you are likely 25 - 50% into the next month already.

## Summary

- Embarking upon continuous improvement through our Program can reap benefits but we need to be able to communicate our results in order to obtain them.
- Those benefits include raises for the workforce, bonuses for your managers, promotions with raises, promotions for yourself, investment in new capital equipment and new customer work being sent to your facility (growth).
- Our communications need to be quantitative in nature with qualitative explanations on how we achieved those metrics.
- For further relevance, we need to match our report to our audience and the forums in which the information is presented: Weekly operations calls, Monthly results calls, Quarterly business reviews, Annual budget meetings and When the boss's boss comes to town.

## Take Away Tool: Monthly Results Call Report
### Manager Update
### January Results Call Agenda

- Sales report
  a. Revenue: actual vs budget vs prior year
  b. Variance explanation to budget and prior year
  c. New customers
  d. Lost customers
  e. Major customer success stories
  f. Customer issues
- Profit report
  a. EBITDA: actual vs budget vs prior year
  b. Variance explanation to budget and prior year
  c. Key Operational Metrics and Reasons for Change
  d. Safety: any recordable or lost time incidents
  e. Waste: waste % vs budget vs py
  f. Quality: any quality issues and the cost of the issues

g. Labor utilization: Labor as a % of revenue vs budget and prior year
h. Turnover rates
- Improvement Projects
  a. Strategic Project 1
     i. Status
     ii. Metrics
  c. Strategic Project 2
     i. Status
     ii. Metrics

# Part 3

## Outsource – How to Find the Right Partner

# CHAPTER 13

# Guide to Outsourcing Kitting and Hand Assembly

## Overheard at your company:

*"So you are going to recruit, train and manage the workforce, provide fixed pricing upfront, hit all of our on-time delivery metrics, meet our quality specifications and save us money?"*

This book has been a collection of process steps in order to turn waste into productivity. I've tried to boil each of them down into discrete modules that can each deliver value independently. Though the real return comes from being able to combine these steps into an overarching program, and a new culture for the hand packaging department. Because running a program takes more time and focus than executing individual phases, this chapter will discuss how to leverage a contract packaging partner to maximize the results that can be achieved as well as speed up the time to achieve those results.

## What is Contract Packaging

Contract packagers (or co-packers) are companies that provide outsourced packaging services to manufacturing companies. Packaging services typically mean putting the products in their packaging, for example putting products into retail cartons, cans, bottles, tubes and pouches. Some contract packagers focus on doing this work using automated equipment while other contract packagers focus on doing this work by hand.

## Hand Work

For this book, and specifically this chapter, we are only going to discuss using a contract packager focused on hand work. While both automated and hand work are considered contract packagers, this book is about how to turn the wastes associated with managing large manual labor workforces into productivity and value.

## Paying For Output Instead Of Input

The main benefit of using a contract packager versus doing it yourself -- whether through full/part time employees or utilizing temps through a staffing agency -- is the difference between paying for input and paying for output. Let's look at the breakdown:

*Paying for Input:*
- Pay a $/hour wage for each hour of 'input' needed to complete a project
- Unknown: the amount of hours needed for the project
- Cost Risk: if you go over the amount of hours needed, then the project may go over-budget and even become unprofitable for the plant. Or you may miss the delivery timeline.
- Also could be considered doing a 'cost plus' arrangement whereby you agree to pay the cost of doing the work plus a profit margin for the staffing supplier

*Paying for Output:*
- Pay only for the products produced
- Doesn't matter: how many hours are needed for the project. This risk is on the co-packer's shoulder
- Downside risk: must have a good partner who is trustworthy and can meet delivery time and quality specification
- Also could be considered doing a 'fixed price contract' arranagement whereby the supplier guarantees you a project cost and must execute within that budget to make a profit

"The real return comes from being able to combine these steps."

## On-Site or Off-Site

If you want to go the route of paying for output and end the days of P&L variances on direct labor and temp expense, then the first decision when considering to work with a contract packager is simple.

Namely, it's whether you want a group to work on your plant floor, or you want to send your products to your partner's site. Here are some considerations:

| CONSIDERATIONS | ON-SITE PROGRAM | CO-PACKER SITE |
|---|---|---|
| Cost Per Unit | ● | |
| Transportation cost | ● | |
| Trust | ● | |
| Control | ● | |
| Flexibility | ● | |
| Add Production Capacity | | ● |
| Floor Space Utilization | | ● |
| Frees up Supervisor time | | ● |

While there are financial and operational pros and cons, the decision likely will come down to whether your product can be sent off site at all. Using a co-packer site is typically preferred by companies who are space capacity constrained.

When work is sent to a co-packer, it frees up floor space, vastly reduces the size of the on-site workforce, frees up capacity for other types of production, and increases secondary space in everything from parking to break rooms and other facility support areas.

## Negotiating With a Co-Packer

To work with a co-packer, there are several industry standards that you should include in your negotiation.

| INCLUDE IN NEGOTIATION | DESCRIPTION |
|---|---|
| **Cost Per Unit** | <ul><li>You should have a detailed pricing menu for each SKU that is fixed and negotiated before the project.</li><li>Quotes for new products should be completed within 24 hours, if you can provide a sample.</li></ul> |
| **Downtime**<br>*(Only applicable to Client Site Programs)* | <ul><li>Both groups should work together to minimize downtime. Typically, the beginning of a program will have some downtime that should go away within 3 months.</li><li>Because a CPU co-packer is only paid for output, it's your responsibility to keep the lines stocked. You can do this with your own material handlers or the co-packer can do it if they are trained on your systems and can coordinate with your supervisor.</li><li>Expect a downtime charge of $14 - $20/hour (in 2018) which is not meant as a profit center for the co-packer, but serves to cover the cost of idle time and also motivate the client's team to work fast.</li><li>All downtime charges should be approved by the client. If a downtime scenario exists, the co-packer's on-site manager will discuss with his/her client and determine the appropriate remedy. If you as the client don't approve downtime, then your co-packer is paying his team to be idle and likely may have to send people home for the day which makes the role tougher.</li><li>If you have sporadic demand and are uncertain if you can keep the co-packer stocked, you should consider doing your project at the co-packer's site to avoid downtime charges. The co-packer is adept at load balancing all of their client work to smooth out production for their workforce.</li></ul> |
| **Quality Warrants** | <ul><li>Keep in mind that you are only paying for 'good output.' The co-packer is agreeing to a fixed cost per unit for good units. If a product packaged does not meet your quality specifications (assuming of course they have been communicated), then the quality warrants kick in and the rework has to be done by the co-packer at no fee.</li><li>This is a powerful motivator for your co-packing partner to have the highest quality standards.</li></ul> |
| **Delivery Times** | <ul><li>Your co-packer must hit your delivery times. Lead times need to be agreed to up front, as the co-packer is responsible for meeting your deadline regardless of the work schedule. Whether that means working OT, working weekends, or adding a night shift. All these are levers that the co-packer will use, but that you don't need to worry about anymore.</li></ul> |

## Is the fixed unit cost you are being quoted cheaper than doing it in house?

There are a few ways to check if the fixed unit cost you are being quoted is reasonable. Here is how fixed unit cost pricing methodology typically works.

1.   Time Studies
2.   Operations Method

You also need to include the risks:

1.   Overtime risk
2.   Can't get labor in time to meet customer delivery date
3.   Quality risk and having re-dos

And finally the indirect costs:

1.   Workforce recruiting and administration
2.   Downtime
3.   Change-overs
4.   Supervision costs
5.   Floor space
6.   Equipment utilization
7.   Material handling

A good rule of thumb is that your time study pricing represents about 50 - 75% of the cost of a fixed unit price. The reason is that most companies see the percentage of non-productive time of their labor force at about 50% between downtime, change-overs, breaks, rework and equipment reliability So if you do a time study and it takes 40 seconds to do 1 product, the fixed unit cost (at $15/hour) would be $0.33 per unit + the indirect costs and the risks stated above for your business

- 1 product in 40 seconds
- 90 products in 1 hour
- $15/hour burdened cost

- $15/hour divided by 90 units = $0.167 per unit on a time study
- $0.167 per unit x 2 to account for 50% non-productive time in a week = 0.33 per unit actual cost

## Should You Bring in Temps or Bring in a Co-Packer?

| | TEMPS | CO-PACKER |
|---|---|---|
| **Cost** | Pay per hour with a mark-up 1.5x for OT | Pay fixed cost for units produced |
| **Know the Total Spend Up Front** | No - Spend varies based on productivity of workforce | Yes - Spend equals cost per unit x # of units needed, no variation |
| **Pay for Downtime** | Yes, at hourly rate | Yes, at downtime rate |
| **Quality Warrants** | No stake in quality | Yes, only paid for good quality |
| **Requires Supervisor Time** | Yes, supervisors and operators will manage the temp labor force | No, supervision handled by Co-Packer<br>Will liaise with client contact |

## Summary

- Contract packaging companies can be useful partners when trying to capture all of the program benefits.
- The main benefit is that a contract packager can take over a hand packaging department which will free up time for your manager and supervisors. It can also free up significant floor space if the contract packager does work in their own facility.
- With contract packagers, you pay for Output instead of Input. This will save money as well as generate a forecastable expense to lock in margins.
- To align your goals with a contract packager, you should negotiate a fixed unit cost up front, an approval process for downtime, and quality warrants to cover any mistakes.

## About the Author

**Paul Baker** is the CFO of Productiv, Inc. where he works with clients to increase their EBITDA through new approaches to managing labor. Paul is a graduate of The Wharton School, University of Pennsylvania.

www.ingramcontent.com/pod-product-compliance
Lightning Source LLC
Chambersburg PA
CBHW072159170526
45158CB00004BA/1702

* 9 7 8 1 0 8 6 0 0 8 8 4 5 *